The Author just before Leaving for Home.

Over The Top

By An American Soldier Who Went

ARTHUR GUY EMPEY
Machine Gunner, Serving in France

Together with

Tommy's Dictionary of the Trenches

WITH ILLUSTRATIONS

A. L. BURT COMPANY

Publishers   New York

Published by Arrangement with G. P. PUTNAM'S SONS

The Knickerbocker Press, New York

To

MY MOTHER AND MY SISTER

I have had many good comrades as I have journeyed around the world, before the mast and in the trenches, but loyal and true as they were, none have ever done, or could ever do, as much as you have done for me. So as a little token of my gratitude for your love and sacrifice I dedicate this book to you.

FOREWORD

DURING sixteen years of "roughing it," knocking around the world, I have rubbed against the high and low and have had ample opportunity of studying, at close range, many different peoples, their ideals, political and otherwise, their hopes and principles. Through this elbow rubbing, and not from reading, I have become convinced of the nobility, truth, and justice of the Allies' cause, and know their fight to be our fight, because it espouses the principles of the United States of America, democracy, justice, and liberty.

To the average American who has not lived and fought with him, the Englishman appears to be distant, reserved, a slow thinker, and lacking in humor, but from my association with the man who inhabits the British Isles, I find that this opinion is unjust. To me, Tommy Atkins has proved himself to be the best of mates, a pal, and bubbling over with a fine sense of humor, a man with a just cause who is willing to sacrifice everything but honor in the advancement of the same.

v

It is my fondest hope that Uncle Sam and John Bull, arms locked, as mates, good and true, each knowing and appreciating the worth of the other, will wend their way through the years to come, happy and contented in each other's company. So if this poor attempt of mine will, in any way, help to bring Tommy Atkins closer to the doorstep of Uncle Sam, my ambition will have been realized.

Perhaps to some of my readers it will appear that I have written of a great and just cause in a somewhat flippant manner, but I assure them such was not my intention. I have tried to tell my experiences in the language of Tommy sitting on the fire step of a front-line trench on the Western Front—just as he would tell his mate next him what was happening at a different part of the line.

A. G. E.

New York City,
May, 1917.

CONTENTS

vii

Contents

"OVER THE TOP"

Over the Top

CHAPTER I

FROM MUFTI TO KHAKI

IT was in an office in Jersey City. I was sitting
at my desk talking to a Lieutenant of the
Jersey National Guard. On the wall was a big
war map decorated with variously colored little
flags showing the position of the opposing armies
on the Western Front in France. In front of me
on the desk lay a New York paper with big flaring
head lines:

LUSITANIA SUNK! AMERICAN LIVES LOST!

The windows were open and a feeling of spring
pervaded the air. Through the open windows
came the strains of a hurdy-gurdy playing

in the street—*I Didn't Raise my Boy to be a Soldier*.

"*Lusitania* Sunk! American Lives Lost!"— *I Didn't Raise my Boy to be a Soldier*. To us these did not seem to jibe.

The Lieutenant in silence opened one of the lower drawers of his desk and took from it an American flag which he solemnly draped over the war map on the wall. Then, turning to me with a grim face, said:

"How about it, Sergeant? You had better get out the muster roll of the Mounted Scouts, as I think they will be needed in the course of a few days."

We busied ourselves till late in the evening writing out emergency telegrams for the men to report when the call should come from Washington. Then we went home.

I crossed over to New York, and as I went up Fulton Street to take the Subway to Brooklyn, the lights in the tall buildings of New York seemed to be burning brighter than usual, as if they, too, had read "*Lusitania* Sunk! American Lives Lost!" They seemed to be glowing with anger and righteous indignation, and their rays wigwagged the message, "REPAY!"

Months passed, the telegrams lying handy, but covered with dust. Then, one momentous morning the Lieutenant with a sigh of disgust removed the flag from the war map and returned to his desk. I immediately followed this action by throwing the telegrams into the wastebasket. Then we looked at each other in silence. He was squirming in his chair and I felt depressed and uneasy.

The telephone rang and I answered it. It was a business call for me requesting my services for an out-of-town assignment. Business was not very good, so this was very welcome. After listening to the proposition, I seemed to be swayed by a peculiarly strong force within me, and answered, "I am sorry that I cannot accept your offer, but I am leaving for England next week," and hung up the receiver. The Lieutenant swung around in his chair, and stared at me in blank astonishment. A sinking sensation came over me, but I defiantly answered his look with, "Well, it's so. I'm going." And I went.

The trip across was uneventful. I landed at Tilbury, England, then got into a string of matchbox cars and proceeded to London, arriving there about 10 P.M. I took a room in a hotel near St. Pancras Station for "five and six—fire extra."

The room was minus the fire, but the "extra"
seemed to keep me warm. That night there was
a Zeppelin raid, but I didn't see much of it,
because the slit in the curtains was too small
and I had no desire to make it larger. Next
morning the telephone bell rang, and someone
asked, "Are you there?" I was, hardly. Anyway, I learned that the Zeps had returned to
their Fatherland, so I went out into the street
expecting to see scenes of awful devastation and
a cowering populace, but everything was normal.
People were calmly proceeding to their work
Crossing the street, I accosted a Bobbie with:

"Can you direct me to the place of damage?"

He asked me, "What damage?"

In surprise, I answered, "Why, the damage
caused by the Zeps."

With a wink, he replied:

"There was no damage, we missed them again."

After several fruitless inquiries of the passers-
by, I decided to go on my own in search of ruined
buildings and scenes of destruction. I boarded
a bus which carried me through Tottenham Court
Road. Recruiting posters were everywhere. The
one that impressed me most was a life-size picture
of Lord Kitchener with his finger pointing directly

at me, under the caption of "Your King and
Country Need You." No matter which way I
turned, the accusing finger followed me. I was
an American, in mufti, and had a little American
flag in the lapel of my coat. I had no king, and
my country had seen fit not to need me, but still
that pointing finger made me feel small and ill at
ease. I got off the bus to try to dissipate this
feeling by mixing with the throng of the sidewalks.

Presently I came to a recruiting office. Inside,
sitting at a desk was a lonely Tommy Atkins.
I decided to interview him in regard to joining
the British Army. I opened the door. He looked
up and greeted me with "I s'y, myte, want to
tyke on?"

I looked at him and answered, "Well, whatever
that is, I'll take a chance at it."

Without the aid of an interpreter, I found out
that Tommy wanted to know if I cared to join
the British Army. He asked me: "Did you ever
hear of the Royal Fusiliers?" Well, in London
you know, Yanks are supposed to know everything,
so I was not going to appear ignorant and answered,
"Sure."

After listening for one half-hour to Tommy's
tale of their exploits on the firing line, I decided

to join. Tommy took me to the recruiting headquarters where I met a typical English Captain. He asked my nationality. I immediately pulled out my American passport and showed it to him. It was signed by Lansing,— Bryan had lost his job a little while previously. After looking at the passport, he informed me that he was sorry but could not enlist me, as it would be a breach of neutrality. I insisted that I was not neutral, because to me it seemed that a real American could not be neutral when big things were in progress, but the Captain would not enlist me.

With disgust in my heart I went out in the street. I had gone about a block when a recruiting Sergeant who had followed me out of the office tapped me on the shoulder with his swagger stick and said: "S'y, I can get you in the Army. We have a 'Leftenant' down at the other office who can do anything. He has just come out of the O. T. C. (Officers' Training Corps) and does not know what neutrality is." I decided to take a chance, and accepted his invitation for an introduction to the Lieutenant. I entered the office and went up to him, opened up my passport, and said:

"Before going further I wish to state that I am an American, not too proud to fight, and want to join your army."

He looked at me in a nonchalant manner, and answered, "That's all right, we take anything over here."

I looked at him kind of hard and replied, "So I notice," but it went over his head.

He got out an enlistment blank, and placing his finger on a blank line said, "Sign here."

I answered, "Not on your tintype."

"I beg your pardon?"

Then I explained to him that I would not sign it without first reading it. I read it over and signed for duration of war. Some of the recruits were lucky. *They signed for seven years only.*

Then he asked me my birthplace. I answered, "Ogden, Utah."

He said, "Oh yes, just outside of New York?"

With a smile, I replied, "Well, it's up the State a little."

Then I was taken before the doctor and passed as physically fit, and was issued a uniform. When I reported back to the Lieutenant, he suggested that, being an American, I go on recruiting service and try to shame some of the slackers into joining the Army.

"All you have to do," he said, "is to go out on the street, and when you see a young fellow in mufti who looks physically fit, just stop him and give him this kind of a talk: 'Aren't you ashamed of yourself, a Britisher, physically fit, and in mufti when your King and Country need you? Don't you know that your country is at war and that the place for every young Briton is on the firing line? Here I am, an American, in khaki, who came four thousand miles to fight for your King and Country, and you, as yet, have not enlisted. Why don't you join? Now is the time.'

"This argument ought to get many recruits, Empey, so go out and see what you can do."

He then gave me a small rosette of red, white, and blue ribbon, with three little streamers hanging down. This was the recruiting insignia and was to be worn on the left side of the cap.

Armed with a swagger stick and my patriotic rosette I went out into Tottenham Court Road in quest of cannon fodder.

Two or three poorly dressed civilians passed me, and although they appeared physically fit,

I said to myself, "They don't want to join the army; perhaps they have someone dependent on them for support," so I did not accost them.

Coming down the street I saw a young dandy, top hat and all, with a fashionably dressed girl walking beside him. I muttered, "You are my meat," and when he came abreast of me I stepped directly in his path and stopped him with my swagger stick, saying:

"You would look fine in khaki, why not change that top hat for a steel helmet? Aren't you ashamed of yourself, a husky young chap like you in mufti when men are needed in the trenches? Here I am, an American, came four thousand miles from Ogden, Utah, just outside of New York, to fight for *your* King and Country. Don't be a slacker, buck up and get into uniform; come over to the recruiting office and I'll have you enlisted."

He yawned and answered, "I don't care if you came forty thousand miles, no one asked you to," and he walked on. The girl gave me a sneering look; I was speechless.

I recruited for three weeks and nearly got one recruit.

This perhaps was not the greatest stunt in the

world, but it got back at the officer who had told
me, "Yes, we take anything over here." I had
been spending a good lot of my recruiting time
in the saloon bar of the "Wheat Sheaf" pub
(there was a very attractive blonde barmaid,
who helped kill time—I was not as serious in
those days as I was a little later when I reached
the front)—well, it was the sixth day and my
recruiting report was blank. I was getting low
in the pocket—barmaids haven't much use
for anyone who cannot buy drinks—so I looked
around for recruiting material. You know a man
on recruiting service gets a "bob" or shilling for
every recruit he entices into joining the army, the
recruit is supposed to get this, but he would not
be a recruit if he were wise to this fact, would he?

Down at the end of the bar was a young fellow
in mufti who was very patriotic—he had about
four "Old Six" ales aboard. He asked me if he
could join, showed me his left hand, two fingers
were missing, but I said that did not matter as
"we take anything over here." The left hand is
the rifle hand as the piece is carried at the slope
on the left shoulder. Nearly everything in
England is "by the left," even general traffic
keeps to the port side.

I took the applicant over to headquarters where he was hurriedly examined. Recruiting surgeons were busy in those days and did not have much time for thorough physical examinations. My recruit was passed as "fit" by the doctor and turned over to a Corporal to make note of his scars. I was mystified. Suddenly the Corporal burst out with, "Blime me, two of his fingers are gone"; turning to me he said, "You certainly have your nerve with you, not 'alf you ain't, to bring this beggar in."

The doctor came over and exploded, "What do you mean by bringing in a man in this condition?"

Looking out of the corner of my eye I noticed that the officer who had recruited me had joined the group, and I could not help answering, "Well, sir, I was told that you took anything over here."

I think they called it "Yankee impudence," anyhow it ended my recruiting.

CHAPTER II

BLIGHTY TO REST BILLETS

THE next morning, the Captain sent for me and informed me: "Empey, as a recruiting Sergeant you are a washout," and sent me to a training depot.

After arriving at this place, I was hustled to the quartermaster stores and received an awful shock. The Quartermaster Sergeant spread a waterproof sheet on the ground, and commenced throwing a miscellaneous assortment of straps, buckles, and other paraphernalia into it. I thought he would never stop, but when the pile reached to my knees he paused long enough to say, "Next, No. 5217, 'Arris, 'B' Company." I gazed in bewilderment at the pile of junk in front of me, and then my eyes wandered around looking for the wagon which was to carry it to the barracks. I was rudely brought to earth by the "Quarter" exclaiming, "'Ere, you, 'op it, tyke it aw'y; blind my eyes, 'e's looking for 'is batman to 'elp 'im carry it."

Struggling under the load, with frequent pauses for rest, I reached our barracks (large car barns), and my platoon leader came to the rescue. It was a marvel to me how quickly he assembled the equipment. After he had completed the task, he showed me how to adjust it on my person. Pretty soon I stood before him a proper Tommy Atkins in heavy marching order, feeling like an overloaded camel.

On my feet were heavy-soled boots, studded with hobnails, the toes and heels of which were reinforced by steel half-moons. My legs were encased in woolen puttees, olive drab in color, with my trousers overlapping them at the top. Then a woolen khaki tunic, under which was a bluish-gray woolen shirt, minus a collar, beneath this shirt a woolen belly-band about six inches wide, held in place by tie strings of white tape. On my head was a heavy woolen trench cap, with huge ear laps buttoned over the top. Then the equipment: A canvas belt, with ammunition pockets, and two wide canvas straps like suspenders, called "D" straps, fastened to the belt in front, passing over each shoulder, crossing in the middle

of my back, and attached by buckles to the rear
of the belt.   On the right side of the belt hung a
water bottle, covered with felt; on the left side was
my bayonet and scabbard, and entrenching tool
handle, this handle strapped to the bayonet
scabbard.   In the rear was my entrenching tool,
carried in a canvas case.   This tool was a combination pick and spade.   A canvas haversack was
strapped to the left side of the belt, while on my
back was the pack, also of canvas, held in place by
two canvas straps over the shoulders; suspended
on the bottom of the pack was my mess tin or
canteen in a neat little canvas case.   My waterproof sheet, looking like a jelly roll, was strapped
on top of the pack, with a wooden stick for cleaning the breach of the rifle projecting from each
end.   On a lanyard around my waist hung a huge
jackknife with a can-opener attachment.   The
pack contained my overcoat, an extra pair of socks,
change of underwear, hold-all (containing knife,
fork, spoon, comb, toothbrush, lather brush, shav-
ing soap, and a razor made of tin, with "Made in
England" stamped on the blade; when trying to
shave with this it made you wish that you were
at war with Patagonia, so that you could have a
"hollow ground" stamped "Made in Germany");

then your housewife, button-cleaning outfit, consisting of a brass button stick, two stiff brushes, and a box of "Soldiers' Friend" paste; then a shoe brush and a box of dubbin, a writing pad, indelible pencil, envelopes, and pay book, and personal belongings, such as a small mirror, a decent razor, and a sheaf of unanswered letters, and fags. In your haversack you carry your iron rations, meaning a tin of bully beef, four biscuits, and a can containing tea, sugar, and Oxo cubes; a couple of pipes and a package of shag, a tin of rifle oil, and a pull-through. Tommy generally carries the oil with his rations; it gives the cheese a sort of sardine taste.

Add to this a first-aid pouch and a long ungainly rifle patterned after the Daniel Boone period, and you have an idea of a British soldier in Blighty.

Before leaving for France, this rifle is taken from him and he is issued with a Lee–Enfield short-trench rifle and a ration bag.

In France he receives two gas helmets, a sheep-skin coat, rubber mackintosh, steel helmet, two blankets, tear-shell goggles, a balaclava helmet, gloves, and a tin of anti-frostbite grease which is excellent for greasing the boots. Add to this the

weight of his rations, and can you blame Tommy
for growling at a twenty kilo route march?

Having served as Sergeant-Major in the United
States Cavalry, I tried to tell the English drill
sergeants their business but it did not work. They
immediately put me as batman in their mess.
Many a greasy dish of stew was accidentally spilled
over them.

I would sooner fight than be a waiter, so when
the order came through from headquarters calling for a draft of 250 reinforcements for France, I
volunteered.

Then we went before the M. O. (Medical Officer)
for another physical examination. This was very
brief. He asked our names and numbers and said,
"Fit," and we went out to fight.

We were put into troop trains and sent to Southampton, where we detrained, and had our trench
rifles issued to us. Then in columns of twos we
went up the gangplank of a little steamer lying
alongside the dock.

At the head of the gangplank there was an old
Sergeant who directed that we line ourselves along
both rails of the ship. Then he ordered us to take
life belts from the racks overhead and put them
on. I have crossed the ocean several times and

knew I was not seasick, but when I buckled on that life belt, I had a sensation of sickness.

After we got out into the stream all I could think of was that there were a million German submarines with a torpedo on each, across the warhead of which was inscribed my name and address.

After five hours we came alongside a pier and disembarked. I had attained another one of my ambitions. I was "somewhere in France." We slept in the open that night on the side of a road. About six the next morning we were ordered to entrain. I looked around for the passenger coaches, but all I could see on the siding were cattle cars. We climbed into these. On the side of each car was a sign reading "Hommes 40, Chevaux 8." When we got inside of the cars, we thought that perhaps the sign painter had reversed the order of things. After forty-eight hours in these trucks we detrained at Rouen. At this place we went through an intensive training for ten days.

This training consisted of the rudiments of trench warfare. Trenches had been dug, with barbed-wire entanglements, bombing saps, dugouts, observation posts, and machine-gun emplacements. We were given a smattering of trench cooking, sanitation, bomb throwing, reconnoiter-

2

ing, listening posts, constructing and repairing
barbed wire, "carrying in" parties, methods used
in attack and defense, wiring parties, mass formation, and the procedure for poison-gas attacks.

On the tenth day we again met our friends
"Hommes 40, Chevaux 8." Thirty-six hours
more of misery, and we arrived at the town of
F——.

After unloading our rations and equipment,
we lined up on the road in columns of fours waiting for the order to march.

A dull rumbling could be heard. The sun was
shining. I turned to the man on my left and
asked, "What's the noise, Bill?" He did not
know, but his face was of a pea-green color. Jim
on my right also did not know, but suggested that
I "awsk" the Sergeant.

Coming towards us was an old grizzled Sergeant,
properly fed up with the war, so I "awsked" him.

"Think it's going to rain, Sergeant?"

He looked at me in contempt, and grunted,
"'Ow's it a'goin' ter rain with the bloomin' sun
a 'shinin'?" I looked guilty.

"Them's the guns up the line, me lad, and
you'll get enough of 'em before you gets back to
Blighty."

My knees seemed to wilt, and I squeaked out a weak "Oh!"

Then we started our march up to the line in ten kilo treks. After the first day's march we arrived at our rest billets. In France they call them rest billets, because while in them, Tommy works seven days a week and on the eighth day of the week he is given twenty-four hours "on his own."

Our billet was a spacious affair, a large barn on the left side of the road, which had one hundred entrances, ninety-nine for shells, rats, wind, and rain, and the hundredth one for Tommy. I was tired out, and using my shrapnel-proof helmet, (shrapnel proof until a piece of shrapnel hits it), or tin hat, for a pillow, lay down in the straw, and was soon fast asleep. I must have slept about two hours, when I awoke with a prickling sensation all over me. As I thought, the straw had worked through my uniform. I woke up the fellow lying on my left, who had been up the line before, and asked him,

"Does the straw bother you, mate? It's worked through my uniform and I can't sleep."

In a sleepy voice, he answered, "That ain't straw, them's cooties."

From that time on my friends the "cooties" were constantly with me.

"Cooties," or body lice, are the bane of Tommy's existence.

The aristocracy of the trenches very seldom call them "cooties," they speak of them as fleas.

To an American, flea means a small insect armed with a bayonet, who is wont to jab it into you and then hop, skip, and jump to the next place to be attacked. There is an advantage in having fleas on you instead of "cooties" in that in one of his extended jumps said flea is liable to land on the fellow next to you; he has the typical energy and push of the American, while the "cootie" has the bulldog tenacity of the Englishman, he holds on and consolidates or digs in until his meal is finished.

There is no way to get rid of them permanently. No matter how often you bathe, and that is not very often, or how many times you change your underwear, your friends, the "cooties" are always in evidence. The billets are infested with them, especially so, if there is straw on the floor.

I have taken a bath and put on brand-new underwear; in fact, a complete change of uniform, and then turned in for the night. The next morning my shirt would be full of them. It is a common sight to see eight or ten soldiers sitting under a tree with their shirts over their knees engaging in a "shirt hunt."

At night about half an hour before "lights out," you can see the Tommies grouped around a candle, trying, in its dim light, to rid their underwear of the vermin. A popular and very quick method is to take your shirt and drawers, and run the seams back and forward in the flame from the candle and burn them out. This practice is dangerous, because you are liable to burn holes in the garments if you are not careful.

Recruits generally sent to Blighty for a brand of insect powder advertised as "Good for body lice." The advertisement is quite right; the powder is good for "cooties," they simply thrive on it.

The older men of our battalion were wiser and made scratchers out of wood. These were rubbed smooth with a bit of stone or sand to prevent splinters. They were about eighteen inches long, and Tommy guarantees that a scratcher of this length will reach any part of the body which may be attacked. Some of the fellows were lazy and only made their scratchers twelve inches, but many a night when on guard, looking over the top from the fire step of the front-line trench, they would have given a thousand "quid" for the other six inches.

Once while we were in rest billets an Irish Hussar regiment camped in an open field opposite our billet. After they had picketed and fed their horses, a general shirt hunt took place. The troopers ignored the call "Dinner up," and kept on with their search for big game. They had a curious method of procedure. They hung their shirts over a hedge and beat them with their entrenching tool handles.

I asked one of them why they didn't pick them off by hand, and he answered, "We haven't had a bath for nine weeks or a change of clabber. If I tried to pick the 'cooties' off my shirt, I would be here for duration of war." After taking a close look at his shirt, I agreed with him, it was alive.

The greatest shock a recruit gets when he arrives at his battalion in France is to see the men engaging in a "cootie" hunt. With an air of contempt and disgust he avoids the company of the older men, until a couple of days later, in a torment of itching, he also has to resort to a shirt hunt, or spend many a sleepless night of misery. During these hunts there are lots of pertinent remarks bandied back and forth among the explorers, such as, "Say, Bill, I'll swap you two little ones for a big one," or, "I've got a black one here that looks like Kaiser Bill."

One sunny day in the front-line trench, I saw three officers sitting outside of their dugout ("cooties" are no respecters of rank; I have even noticed a suspicious uneasiness about a certain well-known general), one of them was a major, two of them were exploring their shirts, paying no attention to the occasional shells which passed overhead. The major was writing a letter; every now and then he would lay aside his writing-pad, search his shirt for a few minutes, get an inspiration, and then resume writing. At last he finished his letter and gave it to his "runner." I was curious to see whether he was writing to an insect firm, so when the runner passed me I engaged him in conversation and got a glimpse at the address on the envelope. It was addressed to Miss Alice Somebody, in London. The "runner" informed me that Miss Somebody was the major's sweetheart and that he wrote to her every day. Just imagine it, writing a love letter during a "cootie" hunt; but such is the creed of the trenches.

CHAPTER III

I GO TO CHURCH

UPON enlistment we had identity disks issued to us. These were small disks of red fiber worn around the neck by means of a string. Most of the Tommies also used a little metal disk which they wore around the left wrist by means of a chain. They had previously figured it out that if their heads were blown off, the disk on the left wrist would identify them. If they lost their left arm the disk around the neck would serve the purpose, but if their head and left arm were blown off, no one would care who they were, so it did not matter. On one side of the disk was inscribed your rank, name, number, and battalion, while on the other was stamped your religion.

C. of E., meaning Church of England; R. C., Roman Catholic; W., Wesleyan; P., Presbyterian; but if you happened to be an atheist they left it blank, and just handed you a pick and shovel.

24

On my disk was stamped C. of E. This is how I got it: The Lieutenant who enlisted me asked my religion. I was not sure of the religion of the British Army, so I answered, "Oh, any old thing," and he promptly put down C. of E.

Now, just imagine my hard luck. Out of five religions I was unlucky enough to pick the only one where church parade was compulsory!

The next morning was Sunday. I was sitting in the billet writing home to my sister telling her of my wonderful exploits while under fire—all recruits do this. The Sergeant-Major put his head in the door of the billet and shouted: "C. of E. outside for church parade!"

I kept on writing. Turning to me, in a loud voice, he asked, "Empey, aren't you C. of E.?"

I answered, "Yep."

In an angry tone, he commanded, "Don't you 'yep' me. Say, 'Yes, Sergeant-Major.'"

I did so. Somewhat mollified, he ordered, "Outside for church parade."

I looked up and answered, "I am not going to church this morning."

He said, "Oh, yes, you are!"

I answered, "Oh, no, I'm not!"—But I went.

We lined up outside with rifles and bayonets,

120 rounds of ammunition, wearing our tin hats, and the march to church began. After marching about five kilos, we turned off the road into an open field. At one end of this field the Chaplain was standing in a limber. We formed a semi-circle around him. Over head there was a black speck circling round and round in the sky. This was a German Fokker. The Chaplain had a book in his left hand—left eye on the book—right eye on the aeroplane. We Tommies were lucky, we had no books, so had both eyes on the aeroplane.

After church parade we were marched back to our billets, and played football all afternoon.

CHAPTER IV

"INTO THE TRENCH"

THE next morning the draft was inspected by our General, and we were assigned to different companies. The boys in the Brigade had nicknamed this general Old Pepper, and he certainly earned the sobriquet. I was assigned to B Company with another American named Stewart.

For the next ten days we "rested," repairing roads for the Frenchies, drilling, and digging bombing trenches.

One morning we were informed that we were going up the line, and our march began.

It took us three days to reach reserve billets— each day's march bringing the sound of the guns nearer and nearer. At night, way off in the distance we could see their flashes, which lighted up the sky with a red glare.

Against the horizon we could see numerous observation balloons or "sausages" as they are called.

On the afternoon of the third day's march I witnessed my first aeroplane being shelled. A thrill ran through me and I gazed in awe. The aeroplane was making wide circles in the air, while little puffs of white smoke were bursting all around it. These puffs appeared like tiny balls of cotton while after each burst could be heard a dull "plop." The Sergeant of my platoon informed us that it was a German aeroplane and I wondered how he could tell from such a distance because the plane seemed like a little black speck in the sky. I expressed my doubt as to whether it was English, French, or German. With a look of contempt he further informed us that the allied anti-aircraft shells when exploding emitted white smoke while the German shells gave forth black smoke, and, as he expressed it, "It must be an Allemand because our pom-poms are shelling, and I know our batteries are not off their bally nappers and are certainly not *strafeing* our own planes, and another piece of advice—don't chuck your weight about until you've been up the line and learnt something."

I immediately quit "chucking my weight about" from that time on.

Just before reaching reserve billets we were

marching along, laughing, and singing one of Tommy's trench ditties—

"I want to go home, I want to go home,
  I don't want to go to the trenches no more
  Where sausages and whizz-bangs are galore.
  Take me over the sea, where the Allemand can't get
    at me,
  Oh, my, I don't want to die,
  I want to go home"—

when overhead came a "swish" through the air, rapidly followed by three others. Then about two hundred yards to our left in a large field, four columns of black earth and smoke rose into the air, and the ground trembled from the report,—the explosion of four German five-nine's, or "coalboxes." A sharp whistle blast, immediately followed by two short ones, rang out from the head of our column. This was to take up "artillery formation." We divided into small squads and went into the fields on the right and left of the road, and crouched on the ground. No other shells followed this salvo. It was our first baptism by shell fire. From the waist up I was all enthusiasm, but from there down, everything was missing. I thought I should die with fright.

After awhile, we re-formed into columns of fours, and proceeded on our way.

About five that night, we reached the ruined village of H——, and I got my first sight of the awful destruction caused by German Kultur.

Marching down the main street we came to the heart of the village, and took up quarters in shell-proof cellars (shell proof until hit by a shell). Shells were constantly whistling over the village and bursting in our rear, searching for our artillery.

These cellars were cold, damp, and smelly, and overrun with large rats—big black fellows. Most of the Tommies slept with their overcoats over their faces. I did not. In the middle of the night I woke up in terror. The cold, clammy feet of a rat had passed over my face. I immediately smothered myself in my overcoat, but could not sleep for the rest of that night.

Next evening, we took over our sector of the line. In single file we wended our way through a zigzag communication trench, six inches deep with mud. This trench was called "Whiskey Street." On our way up to the front line an occasional flare of bursting shrapnel would light up the sky and we could hear the fragments slapping the ground above us on our right and left. Then a Fritz

Diagram Showing Typical Front-Line and Communication Trenches.

would traverse back and forth with his "type-writer" or machine gun. The bullets made a sharp cracking noise overhead.

The boy in front of me named Prentice crumpled up without a word. A piece of shell had gone through his shrapnel-proof helmet. I felt sick and weak.

In about thirty minutes we reached the front line. It was dark as pitch. Every now and then a German star shell would pierce the blackness out in front with its silvery light. I was trembling all over, and felt very lonely and afraid. All orders were given in whispers. The company we relieved filed past us and disappeared into the blackness of the communication trench leading to the rear. As they passed us, they whispered, "The best o' luck mates."

I sat on the fire step of the trench with the rest of the men. In each traverse two of the older men had been put on guard with their heads sticking over the top, and with their eyes trying to pierce the blackness in "No Man's Land." In this trench there were only two dugouts, and these were used by Lewis and Vickers, machine gunners, so it was the fire step for ours. Pretty soon it started to rain. We put on our "macks," but they were not much protection. The rain trickled down our backs, and it was not long before we were wet and cold. How I passed that night I will never know, but without any unusual occurrence, dawn arrived.

The word "stand down" was passed along the line, and the sentries got down off the fire step. Pretty soon the rum issue came along, and it was a Godsend. It warmed our chilled bodies and put new life into us. Then from the communication trenches came dixies or iron pots, filled with steaming tea, which had two wooden stakes through their handles, and were carried by two men. I filled my canteen and drank the hot tea without taking it from my lips. It was not long before I was asleep in the mud on the fire step.

My ambition had been attained! I was in a front-line trench on the Western Front, and oh, how I wished I were back in Jersey City.

CHAPTER V

MUD, RATS, AND SHELLS

I MUST have slept for two or three hours, not the refreshing kind that results from clean sheets and soft pillows, but the sleep that comes from cold, wet, and sheer exhaustion.

Suddenly, the earth seemed to shake and a thunderclap burst in my ears. I opened my eyes,—I was splashed all over with sticky mud, and men were picking themselves up from the bottom of the trench. The parapet on my left had toppled into the trench, completely blocking it with a wall of tossed-up earth. The man on my left lay still. I rubbed the mud from my face, and an awful sight met my gaze—his head was smashed to a pulp, and his steel helmet was full of brains and blood. A German "Minnie" (trench mortar) had exploded in the next traverse. Men were digging into the soft mass of mud in a frenzy of haste. Stretcher-bearers came up the trench on the double. After a few minutes of digging, three still, muddy forms on stretchers were carried down the communication trench to the rear. Soon they would be resting "somewhere in France," with a little wooden cross over their heads. They had done their bit for King and Country, had died without firing a shot, but their services were appreciated, nevertheless.

Later on, I found out their names. They belonged to our draft.

I was dazed and motionless. Suddenly a shovel was pushed into my hands, and a rough but kindly voice said:

"Here, my lad, lend a hand clearing the trench, but keep your head down, and look out for snipers. One of the Fritz's is a daisy, and he'll get you if you're not careful."

Lying on my belly on the bottom of the trench, I filled sandbags with the sticky mud, they were dragged to my rear by the other men, and the work of rebuilding the parapet was on. The harder I worked, the better I felt. Although the weather was cold, I was soaked with sweat.

Occasionally a bullet would crack overhead, and a machine gun would kick up the mud on the bashed-in parapet. At each crack I would duck and shield my face with my arm. One of the older men noticed this action of mine, and whispered:

"Don't duck at the crack of a bullet, Yank; the danger has passed,—you never hear the one that wings you. Always remember that if you are going to get it, you'll get it, so never worry."

This made a great impression on me at the time, and from then on, I adopted his motto, "If you're going to get it, you'll get it."

It helped me wonderfully. I used it so often afterwards that some of my mates dubbed me, "If you're going to get it, you'll get it."

After an hour's hard work, all my nervousness left me, and I was laughing and joking with the rest.

At one o'clock, dinner came up in the form of a dixie of hot stew.

I looked for my canteen. It had fallen off the fire step, and was half buried in the mud. The man on my left noticed this, and told the Corporal, dishing out the rations, to put my share in his mess tin. Then he whispered to me, "Always take care of your mess tin, mate."

I had learned another maxim of the trenches.

That stew tasted fine. I was as hungry as

a bear. We had "seconds," or another helping, because three of the men had "gone West," killed by the explosion of the German trench mortar, and we ate their share, but still I was hungry, so I filled in with bully beef and biscuits. Then I drained my water bottle. Later on I learned another maxim of the front line,—"Go sparingly with your water." The bully beef made me thirsty, and by tea time I was dying for a drink, but my pride would not allow me to ask my mates for water. I was fast learning the ethics of the trenches.

That night I was put on guard with an older man. We stood on the fire step with our heads over the top, peering out into No Man's Land. It was nervous work for me, but the other fellow seemed to take it as part of the night's routine.

Then something shot past my face. My heart stopped beating, and I ducked my head below the parapet. A soft chuckle from my mate brought me to my senses, and I feebly asked, "For God's sake, what was that?"

He answered, "Only a rat taking a promenade along the sandbags." I felt very sheepish.

About every twenty minutes the sentry in the next traverse would fire a star shell from his flare pistol. The "plop" would give me a start of fright. I never got used to this noise during my service in the trenches.

I would watch the arc described by the star shell, and then stare into No Man's Land waiting for it to burst. In its lurid light the barbed wire and stakes would be silhouetted against its light like a latticed window. Then darkness.

Once, out in front of our wire, I heard a noise and saw dark forms moving. My rifle was lying across the sandbagged parapet. I reached for it, and was taking aim to fire, when my mate grasped my arm, and whispered, "Don't fire." He challenged in a low voice. The reply came back instantly from the dark forms:

"Shut your blinkin' mouth, you bloomin' idiot; do you want us to click it from the Boches?"

Later we learned that the word, "No challenging or firing, wiring party out in front," had been given to the sentry on our right, but he had failed to pass it down the trench. An officer had overheard our challenge and the reply, and immediately put the offending sentry under arrest. The sentry clicked twenty-one days on the wheel, that is, he received twenty-one days' Field Punishment No. I, or "crucifixion," as Tommy terms it.

This consists of being spread-eagled on the wheel of a limber two hours a day for twenty-one days, regardless of the weather. During this period, your rations consist of bully beef, biscuits, and water.

A few months later I met this sentry and he confided to me that since being "crucified," he has never failed to pass the word down the trench when so ordered. In view of the offence, the above punishment was very light, in that failing to pass the word down a trench may mean the loss of many lives, and the spoiling of some important enterprise in No Man's Land.

CHAPTER VI

"BACK OF THE LINE"

OUR tour in the front-line trench lasted four days, and then we were relieved by the —— Brigade.

Going down the communication trench we were in a merry mood, although we were cold and wet, and every bone in our bodies ached. It makes a lot of difference whether you are "going in" or "going out."

At the end of the communication trench, limbers were waiting on the road for us. I thought we were going to ride back to rest billets, but soon found out that the only time an infantry man rides is when he is wounded and is bound for the base or Blighty. These limbers carried our reserve ammunition and rations. Our march to rest billets was thoroughly enjoyed by me. It seemed as if I were on furlough, and was leaving behind everything that was disagreeable and horrible. Every recruit feels this way after being relieved from the trenches.

We marched eight kilos and then halted in front of a French *estaminet*. The Captain gave the order to turn out on each side of the road and wait his return. Pretty soon he came back and told B Company to occupy billets 117, 118, and 119. Billet 117 was an old stable which had previously been occupied by cows. About four feet in front of the entrance was a huge manure pile, and the odor from it was anything but pleasant. Using my flashlight I stumbled through the door. Just before entering I observed a white sign reading: "Sitting 50, lying 20," but, at the time, its significance did not strike me. Next morning I asked the Sergeant-Major what it meant. He nonchalantly answered:

"That's some of the work of the R. A. M. C. (Royal Army Medical Corps). It simply means that in case of an attack, this billet will accommodate fifty wounded who are able to sit up and take notice, or twenty stretcher cases."

It was not long after this that I was one of the "20 lying."

I soon hit the hay and was fast asleep, even my friends the "cooties" failed to disturb me.

The next morning at about six o'clock I was awakened by the Lance-Corporal of our section, informing me that I had been detailed as mess orderly, and to report to the cook to give him a hand. I helped him make the fire, carry water from an old well, and fry the bacon. Lids of dixies are used to cook the bacon in. After breakfast was cooked, I carried a dixie of hot tea and the lid full of bacon to our section, and told the Corporal that breakfast was ready. He looked at me in contempt, and then shouted, "Breakfast up, come and get it!" I immediately got wise to the trench parlance, and never again informed that "Breakfast was served."

It didn't take long for the Tommies to answer this call. Half dressed, they lined up with their canteens and I dished out the tea. Each Tommy carried in his hand a thick slice of bread which had been issued with the rations the night before. Then I had the pleasure of seeing them dig into the bacon with their dirty fingers. The allowance was one slice per man. The late ones received very small slices. As each Tommy got his share, he immediately disappeared into the billet. Pretty soon about fifteen of them made a rush to the cookhouse, each carrying a huge slice of bread.

These slices they dipped into the bacon grease which was stewing over the fire. The last man invariably lost out. I was the last man.

After breakfast, our section carried their equipment into a field adjoining the billet and got busy removing the trench mud therefrom, because at 8.45 A.M., they had to fall in for inspection and parade, and woe betide the man who was unshaven, or had mud on his uniform. Cleanliness is next to Godliness in the British Army, and Old Pepper must have been personally acquainted with St. Peter.

Our drill consisted of close order formation which lasted until noon. During this time we had two ten-minute breaks for rest, and no sooner the word, "Fall out for ten minutes," was given, than each Tommy got out a fag and lighted it.

Fags are issued every Sunday morning, and you generally get between twenty and forty. The brand generally issued is the "Woodbine." Sometimes we are lucky, and get "Goldflakes," "Players," or "Red Hussars." Occasionally an issue of "Life Rays" comes along. Then the older Tommies immediately get busy on the recruits, and trade these for Woodbines or Goldflakes. A recruit only has to be stuck once in this manner, and then he ceases to be a recruit. There is a reason. Tommy is a great cigarette smoker. He smokes under all conditions, except when unconscious or when he is reconnoitering in No Man's Land at night. Then, for obvious reasons, he does not care to have a lighted cigarette in his mouth.

Stretcher-bearers carry fags for wounded Tommies. When a stretcher-bearer arrives alongside of a Tommy who has been hit, the following conversation usually takes place—Stretcher-bearer, "Want a fag? Where are you hit?" Tommy looks up and answers, "Yes. In the leg."

After dismissal from parade, we returned to our billets, and I had to get busy immediately with the dinner issue. Dinner consisted of stew made from fresh beef, a couple of spuds, bully beef, Maconochie rations and water,—plenty of water. There is great competition among the men to spear with their forks the two lonely potatoes.

After dinner I tried to wash out the dixie with cold water and a rag, and learned another maxim of the trenches—"It can't be done." I slyly watched one of the older men from another section, and was horrified to see him throw into his dixie four or five double handfuls of mud.

Then he poured in some water, and with his hands scoured the dixie inside and out. I thought he was taking an awful risk. Supposing the cook should have seen him! After half an hour of unsuccessful efforts, I returned my dixie to the cook shack, being careful to put on the cover, and returned to the billet. Pretty soon the cook poked his head in the door and shouted: "Hey, Yank, come out here and clean your dixie!" I protested that I had wasted a half-hour on it already, and had used up my only remaining shirt in the attempt. With a look of disdain, he exclaimed: "Blow me, your shirt! Why in 'ell didn't you use mud?"

Without a word in reply I got busy with the mud, and soon my dixie was bright and shining.

Most of the afternoon was spent by the men writing letters home. I used my spare time to chop wood for the cook, and go with the Quartermaster to draw coal. I got back just in time to issue our third meal, which consisted of hot tea. I rinsed out my dixie and returned it to the cookhouse, and went back to the billet with an exhilarated feeling that my day's labor was done. I had fallen asleep on the straw when once again the cook appeared in the door of the billet with

"Blime me, you Yanks are lazy. Who in 'ell's a'goin' to draw the water for the mornin' tea? Do you think I'm a'goin' to? Well, I'm not," and he left. I filled the dixie with water from an old squeaking well, and once again lay down in the straw.

CHAPTER VII

RATIONS

JUST before dozing off, Mr. Lance-Corporal
butted in.

In Tommy's eyes, a Lance-Corporal is one
degree below a Private. In the Corporal's eyes,
he is one degree above a General.

He ordered me to go with him and help him draw
the next day's rations, also told me to take my
waterproof.

Every evening, from each platoon or machine-
gun section, a Lance-Corporal and Private goes
to the Quartermaster-Sergeant at the Company
Stores and draws rations for the following day.

The "Quarter," as the Quartermaster-Sergeant
is called, receives daily from the Orderly Room
(Captain's Office) a slip showing the number of
men entitled to rations, so there is no chance of
putting anything over on him. Many arguments
take place between the "Quarter" and the pla-

toon Non-Com, but the former always wins out.
Tommy says the "Quarter" got his job because
he was a burglar in civil life.

Then I spread the waterproof sheet on the
ground, while the Quartermaster's Batman dumped
the rations on it. The Corporal was smoking a
fag. I carried the rations back to the billet. The
Corporal was still smoking a fag. How I envied
him. But when the issue commenced my envy
died, and I realized that the first requisite of a
non-commissioned officer on active service is
diplomacy. There were nineteen men in our
section, and they soon formed a semi-circle around
us after the Corporal had called out, "Rations
up."

The Quartermaster-Sergeant had given a slip
to the Corporal on which was written a list of the
rations. Sitting on the floor, using a wooden box
as a table, the issue commenced. On the left of
the Corporal the rations were piled. They consisted of the following:

Six loaves of fresh bread, each loaf of a different
size, perhaps one out of the six being as flat as a
pancake, the result of an Army Service Corps
man placing a box of bully beef on it during transportation.

Three tins of jam, one apple, and the other two plum.

Seventeen Bermuda onions, all different sizes.

A piece of cheese in the shape of a wedge.

Two one-pound tins of butter.

A handful of raisins.

A tin of biscuits, or as Tommy calls them "Jaw-breakers."

A bottle of mustard pickles.

The "bully beef," spuds, condensed milk, fresh meat, bacon, and "Maconochie Rations" (a can filled with meat, vegetables, and greasy water), had been turned over to the Company Cook to make stew for next day's dinner. He also received the tea, sugar, salt, pepper, and flour.

Scratching his head, the Corporal studied the slip issued to him by the Quarter. Then in a slow, mystified voice he read out, "No. 1 Section, 19 men. Bread, loaves, six." He looked puzzled and soliloquized in a musing voice:

"Six loaves, nineteen men. Let's see, that's three in a loaf for fifteen men,—well to make it even, four of you'll have to muck in on one loaf."

The four that got stuck made a howl, but to no avail. The bread was dished out. Pretty soon from a far corner of the billet, three indignant Tommies accosted the Corporal with,

"What do you call this, a loaf of bread? Looks more like a sniping plate."

The Corporal answered:

"Well, don't blame me, I didn't bake it, somebody's got to get it, so shut up until I dish out these blinkin' rations."

Then the Corporal started on the jam.

"Jam, three tins—apple one, plum two. Nineteen men, three tins. Six in a tin, makes twelve men for two tins, seven in the remaining tin."

He passed around the jam, and there was another riot. Some didn't like apple, while others who received plum were partial to apple. After awhile differences were adjusted, and the issue went on.

"Bermuda onions, seventeen."

The Corporal avoided a row by saying that he did not want an onion, and I said they make your breath smell, so guessed I would do without one too. The Corporal looked his gratitude.

"Cheese, pounds two."

The Corporal borrowed a jackknife (corporals are always borrowing), and sliced the cheese,— each slicing bringing forth a pert remark from the on-lookers as to the Corporal's eyesight.

"Raisins, ounces, eight."

By this time the Corporal's nerves had gone West, and in despair, he said that the raisins were to be turned over to the cook for "duff" (plum pudding). This decision elicited a little "grousing," but quiet was finally restored.

"Biscuits, tins, one."

With his borrowed jackknife, the Corporal opened the tin of biscuits, and told everyone to help themselves,—nobody responded to this invitation. Tommy is "fed up" with biscuits.

"Butter, tins, two."

"Nine in one, ten in the other."

Another rumpus.

"Pickles, mustard, bottles, one."

Nineteen names were put in a steel helmet, the last one out winning the pickles. On the next issue there were only eighteen names, as the winner is eliminated until every man in the section has won a bottle.

The raffle is closely watched, because Tommy is suspicious when it comes to gambling with his rations.

When the issue is finished, the Corporal sits down and writes a letter home, asking them if they cannot get some M.P. (Member of Parliament)

to have him transferred to the Royal Flying Corps
where he won't have to issue rations.

At the different French *estaminets* in the village, and at the canteens, Tommy buys fresh eggs,
milk, bread, and pastry. Occasionally when he is
flush, he invests in a tin of pears or apricots. His
pay is only a shilling a day, twenty-four cents, or
a cent an hour. Just imagine, a cent an hour for
being under fire,—not much chance of getting rich
out there.

When he goes into the fire trench (front line),
Tommy's menu takes a tumble. He carries in his
haversack what the government calls emergency
or iron rations. They are not supposed to be
opened until Tommy dies of starvation. They
consist of one tin of bully beef, four biscuits, a
little tin which contains tea, sugar, and Oxo cubes
(concentrated beef tablets). These are only to be
used when the enemy establishes a curtain of shell
fire on the communication trenches, thus prevent-
ing the "carrying in" of rations, or when in an
attack, a body of troops has been cut off from its
base of supplies.

The rations are brought up, at night, by the
Company Transport. This is a section of the
company in charge of the Quartermaster-Sergeant.

composed of men, mules, and limbers (two wheeled wagons), which supplies Tommy's wants while in the front line. They are constantly under shell fire. The rations are unloaded at the entrance to the communication trenches and are "carried in" by men detailed for that purpose. The Quartermaster-Sergeant never goes into the front-line trench. He doesn't have to, and I have never heard of one volunteering to do so.

The Company Sergeant-Major sorts the rations, and sends them in.

Tommy's trench rations consist of all the bully beef he can eat, biscuits, cheese, tinned butter (sometimes seventeen men to a tin), jam, or marmalade, and occasionally fresh bread (ten to a loaf). When it is possible, he gets tea and stew.

When things are quiet, and Fritz is behaving like a gentleman, which seldom happens, Tommy has the opportunity of making dessert. This is "trench pudding." It is made from broken biscuits, condensed milk, jam—a little water added, slightly flavored with mud—put into a canteen and cooked over a little spirit stove known as "Tommy's cooker."

(A firm in Blighty widely advertises these cookers as a necessity for the men in the trenches. Gullible people buy them,—ship them to the Tommies, who, immediately upon receipt of same throw them over the parapet. Sometimes a Tommy falls for the Ad., and uses the cooker in a dugout to the disgust and discomfort of the other occupants.)

This mess is stirred up in a tin and allowed to simmer over the flames from the cooker until Tommy decides that it has reached a sufficient (glue-like) consistency. He takes his bayonet and by means of the handle carries the mess up in the front trench to cool. After it has cooled off he tries to eat it. Generally one or two Tommies in a section have cast-iron stomachs and the tin is soon emptied. Once I tasted trench pudding, but only once.

In addition to the regular ration issue Tommy uses another channel to enlarge his menu.

In the English papers a "Lonely Soldier" column is run. This is for the soldiers at the front who are supposed to be without friends or relatives. They write to the papers and their names are published. Girls and women in England answer them, and send out parcels of foodstuffs, cigarettes, candy, etc. I have known a "lonely" soldier to receive as many as five parcels and eleven letters in one week.

CHAPTER VIII

THE LITTLE WOODEN CROSS

AFTER remaining in rest billets for eight days, we received the unwelcome tidings that the next morning we would "go in" to "take over." At six in the morning our march started and, after a long march down the dusty road, we again arrived at reserve billets.

I was No. 1 in the leading set of 4's. The man on my left was named "Pete Walling," a cheery sort of fellow. He laughed and joked all the way on the march, buoyed up my drooping spirits. I could not figure out anything attractive in again occupying the front line, but Pete did not seem to mind, said it was all in a lifetime. My left heel was blistered from the rubbing of my heavy marching boot. Pete noticed that I was limping and offered to carry my rifle, but by this time I had learned the ethics of the march in the British Army and courteously refused his offer.

We had gotten half-way through the communication trench, Pete in my immediate rear. He had his hand on my shoulder, as men in a communication trench have to keep in touch with each other. We had just climbed over a bashed-in part of the trench when in our rear a man tripped over a loose signal wire, and let out an oath. As usual, Pete rushed to his help. To reach the fallen man, he had to cross this bashed-in part. A bullet cracked in the air and I ducked. Then a moan from the rear. My heart stood still. I went back and Pete was lying on the ground; by the aid of my flashlight, I saw that he had his hand pressed to his right breast. The fingers were covered with blood. I flashed the light on his face, and in its glow a grayish-blue color was stealing over his countenance. Pete looked up at me and said: "Well, Yank, they've done me in. I can feel myself going West." His voice was getting fainter and I had to kneel down to get the words. Then he gave me a message to write home to his mother and his sweetheart, and I, like a great big boob, cried like a baby. I was losing my first friend of the trenches.

Word was passed to the rear for a stretcher. He died before it arrived. Two of us put the body

on the stretcher and carried it to the nearest first-
aid post, where the doctor took an official record
of Pete's name, number, rank, and regiment from
his identity disk, this to be used in the Casualty
Lists and notification to his family.

We left Pete there, but it broke our hearts to do
so. The doctor informed us that we could bury
him the next morning. That afternoon, five of the
boys of our section, myself included, went to the
little ruined village in the rear and from the deserted gardens of the French châteaux gathered
grass and flowers. From these we made a
wreath.

While the boys were making this wreath, I sat
under a shot-scarred apple tree and carved out the
following verses on a little wooden shield which we
nailed on Pete's cross.

> True to his God; true to Britain,
>   Doing his duty to the last,
> Just one more name to be written
>   On the Roll of Honor of heroes passed—
>
> Passed to their God, enshrined in glory,
>   Entering life of eternal rest,
> One more chapter in England's story
>   Of her sons doing their best.

Rest, you soldier, mate so true,
  Never forgotten by us below;
Know that we are thinking of you,
  Ere to our rest we are bidden to go.

Next morning the whole section went over to say good-bye to Pete, and laid him away to rest.

After each one had a look at the face of the dead, a Corporal of the R. A. M. C. sewed up the remains in a blanket. Then placing two heavy ropes across the stretcher (to be used in lowering the body into the grave), we lifted Pete onto the stretcher, and reverently covered him with a large Union Jack, the flag he had died for.

The Chaplain led the way, then came the officers of the section, followed by two of the men carrying a wreath. Immediately after came poor Pete on the flag-draped stretcher, carried by four soldiers. I was one of the four. Behind the stretcher, in column of fours, came the remainder of the section.

To get to the cemetery, we had to pass through the little shell-destroyed village, where troops were hurrying to and fro.

As the funeral procession passed, these troops came to the "attention," and smartly saluted the dead.

Poor Pete was receiving the only salute a Private is entitled to "somewhere in France."

Now and again a shell from the German lines would go whistling over the village to burst in our artillery lines in the rear.

When we reached the cemetery, we halted in front of an open grave, and laid the stretcher beside it. Forming a hollow square around the opening of the grave, the Chaplain read the burial service.

German machine-gun bullets were "cracking" in the air above us, but Pete didn't mind, and neither did we.

When the body was lowered into the grave, the flag having been removed, we clicked our heels together, and came to the salute.

I left before the grave was filled in. I could not bear to see the dirt thrown on the blanket-covered face of my comrade. On the Western Front there are no coffins, and you are lucky to get a blanket to protect you from the wet and the worms. Several of the section stayed and decorated the grave with white stones.

That night, in the light of a lonely candle in the machine-gunner's dugout of the front-line trench, I wrote two letters. One to Pete's mother, the other to his sweetheart. While doing this I cursed the Prussian war-god with all my heart, and I think that St. Peter noted same.

The machine gunners in the dugout were laughing and joking. To them, Pete was unknown. Pretty soon, in the warmth of their merriment, my blues disappeared. One soon forgets on the Western Front.

CHAPTER IX

SUICIDE ANNEX

I WAS in my first dugout and looked around curiously. Over the door of same was a little sign reading, "Suicide Annex." One of the boys told me that this particular front trench was called "Suicide Ditch." Later on I learned that machine gunners and bombers are known as the "Suicide Club."

That dugout was muddy. The men slept in mud, washed in mud, ate mud, and dreamed mud. I had never before realized that so much discomfort and misery could be contained in those three little letters, M U D. The floor of the dugout was an inch deep in water. Outside it was raining cats and dogs, and thin rivulets were trickling down the steps. From the airshaft immediately above me came a drip, drip, drip. Suicide Annex was a hole eight feet wide, ten feet long,

and six feet high. It was about twenty feet below
the fire trench; at least there were twenty steps
leading down to it. These steps were cut into the
earth, but at that time were muddy and slippery.
A man had to be very careful or else he would
"shoot the chutes." The air was foul, and you
could cut the smoke from Tommy's fags with a
knife. It was cold. The walls and roof were
supported with heavy square-cut timbers, while
the entrance was strengthened with sandbags.
Nails had been driven into these timbers. On
each nail hung a miscellaneous assortment of
equipment. The lighting arrangements were
superb—one candle in a reflector made from an
ammunition tin. My teeth were chattering from
the cold, and the drip from the airshaft did not
help matters much. While I was sitting bemoan-
ing my fate, and wishing for the fireside at home,
the fellow next to me, who was writing a letter,
looked up and innocently asked, "Say, Yank, how
do you spell 'conflagration'?"

I looked at him in contempt, and answered
that I did not know.

From the darkness in one of the corners came
a thin, piping voice singing one of the popular
trench ditties entitled:

"Pack up your Troubles in your Old Kit Bag, and
Smile, Smile, Smile."

Every now and then the singer would stop to
Cough, Cough, Cough,

but it was a good illustration of Tommy's cheerful-
ness under such conditions.

A machine-gun officer entered the dugout and
gave me a hard look. I sneaked past him,
sliding, and slipping and reached my section of
the front-line trench where I was greeted by the
Sergeant, who asked me, "Where in 'ell 'ave *you*
been?"

I made no answer, but sat on the muddy fire
step, shivering with the cold and with the rain
beating in my face. About half an hour later
I teamed up with another fellow and went on
guard with my head sticking over the top. At
ten o'clock I was relieved and resumed my sitting
position on the fire step. The rain suddenly
stopped and we all breathed a sigh of relief. We
prayed for the morning and the rum issue.

CHAPTER X

"THE DAY'S WORK"

I WAS fast learning that there is a regular routine about the work of the trenches, although it is badly upset at times by the Germans.

The real work in the fire trench commences at sundown. Tommy is like a burglar, he works at night.

Just as it begins to get dark the word "stand to" is passed from traverse to traverse, and the men get busy. The first relief, consisting of two men to a traverse, mount the fire step, one man looking over the top, while the other sits at his feet, ready to carry messages or to inform the platoon officer of any report made by the sentry as to his observations in No Man's Land. The sentry is not allowed to relax his watch for a second. If he is questioned from the trench or asked his orders, he replies without turning around or taking his eyes from the expanse of dirt in front of him. The remainder of the occupants of his traverse either sit on the fire step, with bayonets fixed, ready for any emergency, or if lucky, and a dugout happens to be in the near vicinity of the traverse, and if the night is quiet, they are permitted to go to same and try and snatch a few winks of sleep. Little sleeping is done; generally the men sit around, smoking fags and seeing who can tell the biggest lie. Some of them perhaps, with their feet in water, would write home sympathizing with the "governor" because he was laid up with a cold, contracted by getting his feet wet on his way to work in Woolwich Arsenal. If a man should manage to doze off, likely as not he would wake with a start as the clammy, cold feet of a rat passed over his face, or the next relief stepped on his stomach while stumbling on their way to relieve the sentries in the trench.

Just try to sleep with a belt full of ammunition around you, your rifle bolt biting into your ribs, entrenching tool handle sticking into the small of your back, with a tin hat for a pillow; and feeling very damp and cold, with "cooties" boring for oil in your arm pits, the air foul from the stench of grimy human bodies and smoke from a juicy pipe being whiffed into your nostrils, then you will not wonder why Tommy occasionally takes a turn in the trench for a rest.

While in a front-line trench orders forbid Tommy from removing his boots, puttees, clothing, or equipment. The "cooties" take advantage of this order and mobilize their forces, and Tommy swears vengeance on them and mutters to himself, "just wait until I hit rest billets and am able to get my own back."

Just before daylight the men "turn to" and tumble out of the dugouts, man the fire step until it gets light, or the welcome order "stand down" is given. Sometimes before "stand down" is ordered, the command "five rounds rapid" is passed along the trench. This means that each man must rest his rifle on the top and fire as rapidly as possible five shots aimed toward the German trenches, and then duck (with the emphasis on the "duck"). There is a great rivalry between the opposing forces to get their rapid fire off first, because the early bird, in this instance, catches the worm,—sort of gets the jump on the other fellow, catching him unawares.

We had a Sergeant in our battalion named Warren. He was on duty with his platoon in the fire trench one afternoon when orders came up

5

from the rear that he had been granted seven days' leave for Blighty, and would be relieved at five o'clock to proceed to England.

He was tickled to death at these welcome tidings and regaled his more or less envious mates beside him on the fire step with the good times in store for him. He figured it out that in two days' time he would arrive at Waterloo Station, London, and then—seven days' bliss!

At about five minutes to five he started to fidget with his rifle, and then suddenly springing up on the fire step with a muttered, "I'll send over a couple of souvenirs to Fritz, so that he'll miss me when I leave," he stuck his rifle over the top and fired two shots, when "crack" went a bullet and he tumbled off the step, fell into the mud at the bottom of the trench, and lay still in a huddled heap with a bullet hole in his forehead.

At about the time he expected to arrive at Waterloo Station he was laid to rest in a little cemetery behind the lines. He had gone to Blighty.

In the trenches one can never tell,—it is not safe to plan very far ahead.

After "stand down" the men sit on the fire step or repair to their respective dugouts and wait for the "rum issue" to materialize. Immediately following the rum, comes breakfast, brought up from the rear. Sleeping is then in order unless some special work turns up.

Around 12.30 dinner shows up. When this is eaten the men try to amuse themselves until "tea" appears at about four o'clock, then "stand to" and they carry on as before.

While in rest billets Tommy gets up about six in the morning, washes up, answers roll call, is inspected by his platoon officer, and has breakfast. At 8.45 he parades (drills) with his company or goes on fatigue according to the orders which have been read out by the Orderly Sergeant the night previous.

Between 11.30 and noon he is dismissed, has his dinner, and is "on his own" for the remainder of the day, unless he has clicked for a digging or working party, and so it goes on from day to day, always "looping the loop" and looking forward to Peace and Blighty.

Sometimes, while engaged in a "cootie" hunt you think. Strange to say, but it is a fact, while Tommy is searching his shirt, serious thoughts come to him. Many a time, when performing this operation, I have tried to figure out the outcome of the war and what will happen to me.

My thoughts generally ran in this channel:

Will I emerge safely from the next attack? If I do, will I skin through the following one, and so on? While your mind is wandering into the future it is likely to be rudely brought to earth by a Tommy interrupting with, "What's good for rheumatism?"

Then you have something else to think of. Will you come out of this war crippled and tied into knots with rheumatism, caused by the wet and mud of trenches and dugouts? You give it up as a bad job and generally saunter over to the nearest *estaminet* to drown your moody forebodings in a glass of sickening French beer, or to try your luck at the always present game of "House." You can hear the sing-song voice of a Tommy droning out the numbers as he extracts the little squares of cardboard from the bag between his feet.

CHAPTER XI

OVER THE TOP

ON my second trip to the trenches our officer was making his rounds of inspection, and we received the cheerful news that at four in the morning we were to go over the top and take the German front-line trench. My heart turned to lead. Then the officer carried on with his instructions. To the best of my memory I recall them as follows: "At eleven a wiring party will go out in front and cut lanes through our barbed wire for the passage of troops in the morning. At two o'clock our artillery will open up with an intense bombardment which will last until four. Upon the lifting of the barrage, the first of the three waves will go over." Then he left. Some of the Tommies, first getting permission from the Sergeant, went into the machine-gunners' dugout, and wrote letters home, saying that in the morning, they were going over the top, and also that if the letters reached

their destination it would mean that the writer
had been killed.

These letters were turned over to the captain
with instructions to mail same in the event of the
writer's being killed. Some of the men made out
their wills in their pay book, under the caption,
"will and last testament."

Then the nerve-racking wait commenced. Every
now and then I would glance at the dial of
my wrist-watch and was surprised to see how fast
the minutes passed by. About five minutes to
two I got nervous waiting for our guns to open up.
I could not take my eyes from my watch. I
crouched against the parapet and strained my
muscles in a death-like grip upon my rifle. As
the hands on my watch showed two o'clock, a
blinding red flare lighted up the sky in our rear,
then thunder, intermixed with a sharp, whistling
sound in the air over our heads. The shells from
our guns were speeding on their way toward the
German lines. With one accord the men sprang
up on the fire step and looked over the top in
the direction of the German trenches. A line of
bursting shells lighted up No Man's Land. The
din was terrific and the ground trembled. Then,
high above our heads we could hear a sighing

moan. Our big boys behind the line had opened up and 9.2's and 15-inch shells commenced dropping into the German lines. The flash of the guns behind the lines, the scream of the shells through the air, and the flare of them, bursting, was a spectacle that put Pain's greatest display into the shade. The constant pup, pup, of German machine guns and an occasional rattle of rifle firing gave me the impression of a huge audience applauding the work of the batteries.

Our eighteen-pounders were destroying the German barbed wire, while the heavier stuff was demolishing their trenches and bashing in dugouts or funk-holes.

Then Fritz got busy.

Their shells went screaming overhead, aimed in the direction of the flares from our batteries. Trench mortars started dropping "Minnies" in our front line. We clicked several casualties. Then they suddenly ceased. Our artillery had taped or silenced them.

During the bombardment you could almost read a newspaper in our trench. Sometimes in the flare of a shell-burst a man's body would be silhouetted against the parados of the trench and it appeared like a huge monster. You could hardly hear yourself think. When an order was to be passed down the trench, you had to yell it, using your hands as a funnel into the ear of the man sitting next to you on the fire step. In about twenty minutes a generous rum issue was doled out. After drinking the rum, which tasted like varnish and sent a shudder through your frame, you wondered why they made you wait until the lifting of the barrage before going over. At ten minutes to four, word was passed down, "Ten minutes to go!" Ten minutes to live! We were shivering all over. My legs felt as if they were asleep. Then word was passed down: "First wave get on and near the scaling ladders."

These were small wooden ladders which we had placed against the parapet to enable us to go over the top on the lifting of the barrage. "Ladders of Death" we called them, and veritably they were.

Before a charge Tommy is the politest of men. There is never any pushing or crowding to be first up these ladders. We crouched around the base of the ladders waiting for the word to go over. I was sick and faint, and was puffing away at an unlighted fag. Then came the word, "Three minutes to go; upon the lifting of the barrage and on the blast of the whistles, 'Over the Top with the Best o' Luck and Give them Hell.' " The famous phrase of the Western Front. The Jonah phrase of the Western Front. To Tommy it means if you are lucky enough to come back, you will be minus an arm or a leg. Tommy hates to be wished the best of luck; so, when peace is declared, if it ever is, and you meet a Tommy on the street, just wish him the best of luck and duck the brick that follows.

I glanced again at my wrist-watch. We all wore them and you could hardly call us "sissies" for doing so. It was a minute to four. I could see the hand move to the twelve, then a dead silence. It hurt. Everyone looked up to see what had happened, but not for long. Sharp whistle blasts rang out along the trench, and with a cheer the men scrambled up the ladders. The bullets were cracking overhead, and occasionally a machine gun would rip and tear the top of the sand bag parapet. How I got up that ladder I will never know. The first ten feet out in front was agony. Then we passed through the lanes in our barbed wire. I knew I was running, but could feel no motion below the waist. Patches on the ground seemed to float to the rear as if I were on a treadmill and scenery was rushing past me. The Germans had put a barrage of shrapnel across No Man's Land, and you could hear the pieces slap the ground about you.

After I had passed our barbed wire and gotten into No Man's Land, a Tommy about fifteen feet to my right front turned around and looking in my direction, put his hand to his mouth and yelled something which I could not make out on account of the noise from the bursting shells. Then he coughed, stumbled, pitched forward, and lay still. His body seemed to float to the rear of me. I could hear sharp cracks in the air about me. These were caused by passing rifle bullets. Frequently, to my right and left, little spurts of dirt would rise into the air, and a ricochet bullet would whine on its way. If a Tommy should see one of these little spurts in front of him, he would tell the nurse about it later. The crossing of No Man's Land remains a blank to me.

Men on my right and left would stumble and fall. Some would try to get up, while others remained huddled and motionless. Then smashed-up barbed wire came into view and seemed carried on a tide to the rear. Suddenly, in front of me loomed a bashed-in trench about four feet wide. Queer-looking forms like mud turtles were scrambling up its wall. One of these forms seemed to slip and then rolled to the bottom of the trench. I leaped across this intervening space. The man to my left seemed to pause in mid-air, then pitched head down into the German trench. I laughed out loud in my delirium. Upon alighting on the other side of the trench I came to with a sudden jolt. Right in front of me loomed a giant form with a rifle which looked about ten feet long, on the end of which seemed seven bayonets. These flashed in the air in front of me. Then through my mind flashed the admonition of our bayonet instructor back in Blighty. He had said, "whenever you get in a charge and run your bayonet up to the hilt into a German, the Fritz will fall. Perhaps your rifle will be wrenched from your grasp. Do not waste time, if the bayonet is fouled in his equipment, by putting your foot on his stomach and tugging at the rifle to extricate the bayonet. Simply press the trigger and the bullet will free it." In my present situation this was fine logic, but for the life of me I could not remember how he had told me to get my bayonet into the German. To me, this was the paramount issue. I closed my eyes, and lunged forward. My rifle was torn from my hands. I must have gotten the German because he had disappeared. About twenty feet to my left front was a huge Prussian nearly six feet four inches in height, a fine specimen of physical manhood. The bayonet from his rifle was missing, but he clutched the barrel in both hands and was swinging the butt around his head. I could almost hear the swish of the butt passing through the air. Three little Tommies were engaged with him. They looked like pigmies alongside of the Prussian. The Tommy on the left was gradually circling to the rear of his opponent. It was a funny sight to see them duck the swinging butt and try to jab him at the same time. The Tommy nearest me received the butt of the German's rifle in a smashing blow below the right temple. It smashed his head like an eggshell. He pitched forward on his side and a convulsive shudder ran through his body. Meanwhile, the other Tommy had gained the rear of the Prussian. Suddenly about four inches of bayonet protruded from the throat of the Prussian soldier, who staggered forward and fell. I will never forget the look of blank astonishment that came over his face.

Then something hit me in the left shoulder and my left side went numb. It felt as if a hot poker was being driven through me. I felt no pain—just a sort of nervous shock. A bayonet had pierced me from the rear. I fell backward on the ground, but was not unconscious, because I could see dim objects moving around me. Then a flash of light in front of my eyes and unconsciousness. Something had hit me on the head. I have never found out what it was.

I dreamed I was being tossed about in an open boat on a heaving sea and opened my eyes. The moon was shining. I was on a stretcher being carried down one of our communication trenches. At the advanced first-aid post my wounds were dressed, and then I was put into an ambulance and sent to one of the base hospitals. The wounds in my shoulder and head were not serious and in six weeks I had rejoined my company for service in the front line.

CHAPTER XII

BOMBING

THE boys in the section welcomed me back, but there were many strange faces. Several of our men had gone West in that charge, and were lying "somewhere in France" with a little wooden cross at their heads. We were in rest billets. The next day, our Captain asked for volunteers for Bombers' School. I gave my name and was accepted. I had joined the Suicide Club, and my troubles commenced. Thirty-two men of the battalion, including myself, were sent to L——, where we went through a course in bombing. Here we were instructed in the uses, methods of throwing, and manufacture of various kinds of hand grenades, from the old "jam tin," now obsolete, to the present Mills bomb, the standard of the British Army.

It all depends where you are as to what you are called. In France they call you a "bomber" and give you medals, while in neutral countries they call you an anarchist and give you "life."

From the very start the Germans were well equipped with effective bombs and trained bomb-throwers, but the English Army was as little prepared in this important department of fighting as in many others. At bombing school an old Sergeant of the Grenadier Guards, whom I had the good fortune to meet, told me of the discouragements this branch of the service suffered before they could meet the Germans on an equal footing. (*Pacifists and small army people in the U. S. please read with care.*) The first English Expeditionary Force had no bombs at all but had clicked a lot of casualties from those thrown by the Boches. One bright morning someone higher up had an idea and issued an order detailing two men from each platoon to go to bombing school to learn the duties of a bomber and how to manufacture bombs. Non-commissioned officers were generally selected for this course. After about two weeks at school they returned to their units in rest billets or in the fire trench as the case might be and got busy teaching their platoons how to make "jam tins."

Previously an order had been issued for all ranks to save empty jam tins for the manufacture of bombs. A Professor of Bombing would sit on the fire step in the front trench with the remainder of his section crowding around to see him work.

On his left would be a pile of empty and rusty jam tins, while beside him on the fire step would be a miscellaneous assortment of material used in the manufacture of the "jam tins."

Tommy would stoop down, get an empty "jam tin," take a handful of clayey mud from the parapet, and line the inside of the tin with this substance. Then he would reach over, pick up his detonator and explosive, and insert them in the tin, the fuse protruding. On the fire step would be a pile of fragments of shell, shrapnel balls, bits of iron, nails, etc.—anything that was hard enough to send over to Fritz; he would scoop up a handful of this junk and put it in the bomb. Perhaps one of the platoon would ask him what he did this for, and he would explain that when the bomb exploded these bits would fly about and kill or wound any German hit by same; the questioner would immediately pull a button off his tunic and hand it to the bomb-maker with, "Well, blime me, send this over as a souvenir," or another Tommy would volunteer an old rusty and broken jackknife; both would be accepted and inserted.

Then the Professor would take another handful of mud and fill the tin, after which he would punch a hole in the lid of the tin and put it over the top of the bomb, the fuse sticking out. Then perhaps he would tightly wrap wire around the outside of the tin and the bomb was ready to send over to Fritz with Tommy's compliments.

A piece of wood about four inches long and two inches wide had been issued. This was to be strapped on the left forearm by means of two leather straps and was like the side of a match box; it was called a "striker." There was a tip like the head of a match on the fuse of the bomb. To ignite the fuse, you had to rub it on the "striker," just the same as striking a match. The fuse was timed to five seconds or longer. Some of the fuses issued in those days would burn down in a second or two, while others would "sizz" for a week before exploding. Back in Blighty the munition workers weren't quite up to snuff, the way they are now. If the fuse took a notion to burn too quickly, they generally buried the bombmaker next day. So making bombs could not be called a "cushy" or safe job.

After making several bombs, the Professor instructs the platoon in throwing them. He takes a "jam tin" from the fire step, trembling a little, because it is nervous work, especially when new at it, lights the fuse on his striker. The fuse begins to "sizz" and sputter and a spiral of smoke, like that from a smouldering fag, rises from it. The platoon splits in two and ducks around the traverse nearest to them. They don't like the looks and sound of the burning fuse. When that fuse begins to smoke and "sizz" you want to say good-bye to it as soon as possible, so Tommy with all his might chucks it over the top and crouches against the parapet, waiting for the explosion.

Lots of times in bombing, the "jam tin" would be picked up by the Germans, before it exploded and thrown back at Tommy with dire results.

After a lot of men went West in this manner, an order was issued, reading something like this:

"To all ranks in the British Army—after igniting the fuse and before throwing the jam tin bomb, count slowly one! two! three!"

This in order to give the fuse time enough to burn down, so that the bomb would explode before the Germans could throw it back.

Tommy read the order—he reads them all, but after he ignited the fuse and it began to smoke,— orders were forgotten, and away she went in record time and back she came to the further discomfort of the thrower.

Then another order was issued to count, "one hundred! two hundred! three hundred!" but Tommy didn't care if the order read to count up to a thousand by quarters he was going to get rid of that "jam tin," because from experience he had learned not to trust it.

When the powers that be realized that they could not change Tommy, they decided to change the type of bomb and did so—substituting the "hair brush," the "cricket-ball," and later the Mills bomb.

The standard bomb used in the British Army is the "Mills." It is about the shape and size of a large lemon. Although not actually a lemon, Fritz insists that it is; perhaps he judges it by the havoc caused by its explosion. The Mills bomb is made of steel, the outside of which is corrugated into forty-eight small squares which, upon the explosion of the bomb, scatter in a wide area, wounding or killing any Fritz who is unfortunate enough to be hit by one of the flying fragments.

Although a very destructive and efficient bomb, the "Mills" has the confidence of the thrower, in that he knows it will not explode until released from his grip.

It is a mechanical device, with a lever, fitted into a slot at the top, which extends half way around the circumference and is held in place at the bottom by a fixing pin. In this pin there is a small metal ring, for the purpose of extracting the pin when ready to throw.

You do not throw a bomb the way a baseball is thrown, because, when in a narrow trench, your hand is liable to strike against the parados, traverse, or parapet, and then down goes the bomb, and, in a couple of seconds or so, up goes Tommy.

In throwing, the bomb and lever are grasped in the right hand, the left foot is advanced, knee stiff, about once and a half its length to the front, while the right leg, knee bent, is carried slightly to the right. The left arm is extended at an angle of 45°, pointing in the direction the bomb is to be thrown. This position is similar to that of shot-putting, only that the right arm is extended downward. Then you hurl the bomb from you with an overhead bowling motion, the same as in cricket, throwing it fairly high in the air, this in order to give the fuse a chance to burn down so that when the bomb lands, it immediately explodes and gives the Germans no time to scamper out of its range or to return it.

As the bomb leaves your hand, the lever, by means of a spring, is projected into the air and falls harmlessly to the ground a few feet in front of the bomber.

When the lever flies off, it releases a strong spring, which forces the firing pin into a percussion cap. This ignites the fuse, which burns down and sets off the detonator, charged with fulminate of mercury, which explodes the main charge of ammonal.

The average British soldier is not an expert at throwing; it is a new game to him, therefore the Canadians and Americans, who have played baseball from the kindergarten up, take naturally to bomb throwing and excel in this act. A six-foot English bomber will stand in awed silence when he sees a little five-foot-nothing Canadian out-distance his throw by several yards. I have read a few war stories of bombing, where baseball pitchers curved their bombs when throwing them, but a pitcher who can do this would make "Christy" Mathewson look like a piker, and is losing valuable time playing in the European War Bush League, when he would be able to set the "Big League" on fire.

We had had a cushy time while at this school.

In fact, to us it was a regular vacation, and we were very sorry when one morning the Adjutant ordered us to report at headquarters for transportation and rations to return to our units up the line.

Arriving at our section, the boys once again tendered us the glad mitt, but looked askance at us out of the corners of their eyes. They could not conceive, as they expressed it, how a man could be such a blinking idiot to join the Suicide Club. I was beginning to feel sorry that I had become a member of said club, and my life to me appeared doubly precious.

Now that I was a sure enough bomber, I was praying for peace and hoping that my services as such would not be required.

CHAPTER XIII

MY FIRST OFFICIAL BATH

RIGHT behind our rest billet was a large creek about ten feet deep and twenty feet across, and it was a habit of the company to avail themselves of an opportunity to take a swim and at the same time thoroughly wash themselves and their underwear when on their own. We were having a spell of hot weather, and these baths to us were a luxury. The Tommies would splash around in the water and then come out and sit in the sun and have what they termed a "shirt hunt." At first we tried to drown the "cooties," but they also seemed to enjoy the bath.

One Sunday morning, the whole section was in the creek and we were having a gay time, when the Sergeant-Major appeared on the scene. He came to the edge of the creek and ordered: "Come out of it. Get your equipment on, 'Drill order,' and fall in for bath parade. Look lively my

hearties. You have only got fifteen minutes."
A howl of indignation from the creek greeted this
order, but out we came. Discipline is discipline.
We lined up in front of our billet with rifles and
bayonets (why you need rifles and bayonets to
take a bath gets me), a full quota of ammunition,
and our tin hats. Each man had a piece of soap
and a towel. After an eight-kilo march along a
dusty road, with an occasional shell whistling
overhead, we arrived at a little squat frame
building upon the bank of a creek. Nailed over
the door of this building was a large sign which
read "Divisional Baths." In a wooden shed in
the rear, we could hear a wheezy old engine pump-
ing water.

We lined up in front of the baths, soaked with
perspiration, and piled our rifles into stacks. A
Sergeant of the R. A. M. C. with a yellow band
around his left arm on which was "S. P." (Sani-
tary Police) in black letters, took charge, ordering
us to take off our equipment, unroll our puttees,
and unlace boots. Then, starting from the right
of the line, he divided us into squads of fifteen.
I happened to be in the first squad.

We entered a small room where we were given
five minutes to undress, then filed into the bath

room. In here there were fifteen tubs (barrels sawed in two) half full of water. Each tub contained a piece of laundry soap. The Sergeant informed us that we had just twelve minutes in which to take our baths. Soaping ourselves all over, we took turns in rubbing each other's backs, then by means of a garden hose, washed the soap off. The water was ice cold, but felt fine.

Pretty soon a bell rang and the water was turned off. Some of the slower ones were covered with soap, but this made no difference to the Sergeant, who chased us into another room, where we lined up in front of a little window, resembling the box office in a theater, and received clean underwear and towels. From here we went into the room where we had first undressed. Ten minutes was allowed in which to get into our "clabber."

My pair of drawers came up to my chin and the shirt barely reached my diaphragm, but they were clean,—no strangers on them, and so I was satisfied.

At the expiration of the time allotted we were turned out and finished our dressing on the grass.

When all of the company had bathed it was a case of march back to billets. That march was the most uncongenial one imagined, just cussing and blinding all the way. We were covered with white dust and felt greasy from sweat. The woolen underwear issued was itching like the mischief.

After eating our dinner of stew, which had been kept for us,—it was now four o'clock,—we went into the creek and had another bath.

If "Holy Joe" could have heard our remarks about the Divisional Baths and army red tape, he would have fainted at our wickedness. But Tommy is only human after all.

I just mentioned "Holy Joe" or the Chaplain in an irreverent sort of way but no offense was meant, as there were some very brave men among them.

There are so many instances of heroic deeds performed under fire in rescuing the wounded that it would take several books to chronicle them, but I have to mention one instance performed by a Chaplain, Captain Hall by name, in the Brigade on our left, because it particularly appealed to me.

A chaplain is not a fighting man; he is recognized as a non-combatant and carries no arms. In a charge or trench raid the soldier gets a feeling of confidence from contact with his rifle, revolver, or bomb he is carrying. He has something to protect himself with, something with which he can inflict harm on the enemy,—in other words, he is able to get his own back.

But the chaplain is empty handed, and is at the mercy of the enemy if he encounters them, so it is doubly brave for him to go over the top, under fire, and bring in wounded. Also a chaplain is not required by the King's Regulations to go over in a charge, but this one did, made three trips under the hottest kind of fire, each time returning with a wounded man on his back. On the third trip he received a bullet through his left arm, but never reported the matter to the doctor until late that night—just spent his time administering to the wants of the wounded lying on stretchers waiting to be carried to the rear by ambulances.

The chaplains in the British Army are a fine, manly set of men, and are greatly respected by Tommy.

CHAPTER XIV

PICKS AND SHOVELS

I HAD not slept long before the sweet voice of the Sergeant informed that "No. 1 Section had clicked for another blinking digging party." I smiled to myself with deep satisfaction. I had been promoted from a mere digger to a member of the Suicide Club, and was exempt from all fatigues. Then came an awful shock. The Sergeant looked over in my direction and said:

"Don't you bomb throwers think that you are wearing top hats out here. 'Cordin' to orders you've been taken up on the strength of this section, and will have to do your bit with the pick and shovel, same as the rest of us."

I put up a howl on my way to get my shovel, but the only thing that resulted was a loss of good humor on my part.

We fell in at eight o'clock, outside of our billets, a sort of masquerade party. I was disguised as a common laborer, had a pick and shovel, and about one hundred empty sandbags. The rest, about two hundred in all, were equipped likewise: picks, shovels, sandbags, rifles, and ammunition.

The party moved out in column of fours, taking the road leading to the trenches. Several times we had to string out in the ditch to let long columns of limbers, artillery, and supplies get past.

The marching, under these conditions, was necessarily slow. Upon arrival at the entrance to the communication trench, I looked at my illuminated wrist-watch—it was eleven o'clock.

Before entering this trench, word was passed down the line, "no talking or smoking, lead off in single file, covering party first."

This covering party consisted of thirty men, armed with rifles, bayonets, bombs, and two Lewis machine guns. They were to protect us and guard against a surprise attack, while digging in No Man's Land.

The communication trench was about half a mile long, a zigzagging ditch, eight feet deep and three feet wide.

Now and again, German shrapnel would whistle overhead and burst in our vicinity. We would crouch against the earthen walls while the shell fragments "slapped" the ground above us.

Once Fritz turned loose with a machine gun, the bullets from which "cracked" through the air and kicked up the dirt on the top, scattering sand and pebbles, which, hitting our steel helmets, sounded like hailstones.

Upon arrival in the fire trench an officer of the Royal Engineers gave us our instructions and acted as guide.

We were to dig an advanced trench two hundred yards from the Germans (the trenches at this point were six hundred yards apart).

Two winding lanes, five feet wide, had been cut through our barbed wire, for the passage of the diggers. From these lanes white tape had been laid on the ground to the point where we were to commence work. This in order that we would not get lost in the darkness. The proposed trench was also laid out with tape.

The covering party went out first. After a short wait, two scouts came back with information that the working party was to follow and "carry on" with their work.

In extended order, two yards apart, we noiselessly crept across No Man's Land. It was ner-

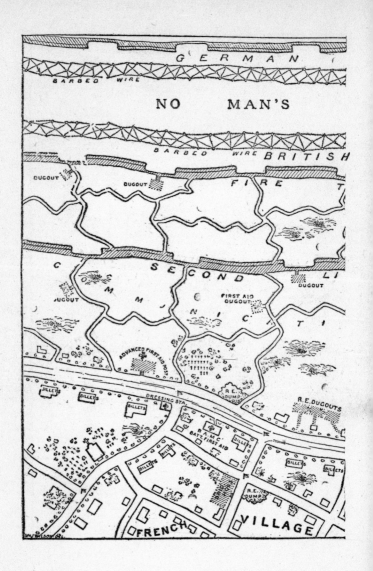

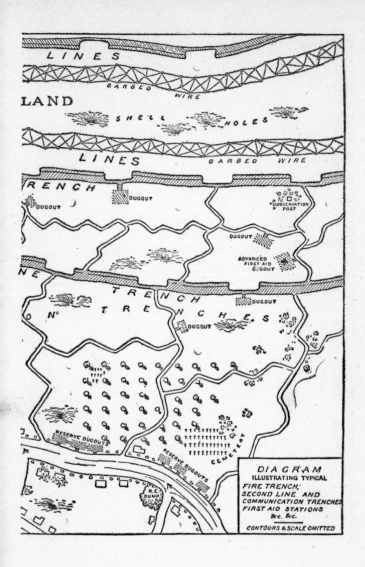

LINES

BARBED WIRE

LAND

SHELL HOLES

LINES

BARBED WIRE

TRENCH

DUGOUT

DUGOUT

OBSERVATION POST

DUGOUT

ADVANCED FIRST AID DUGOUT

NE

TRENCH

TRENCHES

N°

DUGOUT

DUGOUT

RESERVE DUGOUTS

RESERVE DUGOUTS

CEMETERY

F

R.E. DUMP

DIAGRAM
ILLUSTRATING TYPICAL
FIRE TRENCH, SECOND LINE AND
COMMUNICATION TRENCHES
FIRST AID STATIONS
&c. &c.

CONTOURS & SCALE OMITTED

vous work; every minute we expected a machine
gun to open fire on us. Stray bullets "cracked"
around us, or a ricochet sang overhead.

Arriving at the taped diagram of the trench,
rifles slung around our shoulders, we lost no time
in getting to work. We dug as quietly as possible,
but every now and then, the noise of a pick or
shovel striking a stone, would send the cold shivers
down our backs. Under our breaths we heartily
cursed the offending Tommy.

At intervals a star shell would go up from the
German lines and we would remain motionless
until the glare of its white light died out.

When the trench had reached a depth of two
feet, we felt safer, because it would afford us cover
in case we were discovered and fired on.

The digging had been in progress about two
hours, when suddenly, hell seemed to break loose
in the form of machine gun and rifle fire.

We dropped down on our bellies in the shallow
trench, bullets knocking up the ground and
snapping in the air. Then the shrapnel butted in.
The music was hot and Tommy danced.

The covering party was having a rough time of
it; they had no cover; just had to take their
medicine.

Word was passed down the line to beat it for our trenches. We needed no urging; grabbing our tools and stooping low, we legged it across No Man's Land. The covering party got away to a poor start but beat us in. They must have had wings because we lowered the record.

Panting and out of breath, we tumbled into our front-line trench. I tore my hands getting through our wire, but, at the time, didn't notice it; my journey was too urgent.

When the roll was called we found that we had gotten it in the nose for sixty-three casualties.

Our artillery put a barrage on Fritz's front-line and communication trenches and their machine gun and rifle fire suddenly ceased.

Upon the cessation of this fire, stretcher-bearers went out to look for killed and wounded. Next day we learned that twenty-one of our men had been killed and thirty-seven wounded. Five men were missing; lost in the darkness they must have wandered over into the German lines, where they were either killed or captured.

Speaking of stretcher-bearers and wounded, it is very hard for the average civilian to comprehend the enormous cost of taking care of wounded and the war in general. He or she gets so accustomed to seeing billions of dollars in print that the significance of the amount is passed over without thought.

From an official statement published in one of the London papers, it is stated that it costs between six and seven thousand pounds ($30,000 to $35,000) to kill or wound a soldier. This result was attained by taking the cost of the war to date and dividing it by the killed and wounded.

It may sound heartless and inhuman, but it is a fact, nevertheless, that from a military standpoint it is better for a man to be killed than wounded.

If a man is killed he is buried, and the responsibility of the government ceases, excepting for the fact that his people receive a pension. But if a man is wounded it takes three men from the firing line, the wounded man and two men to carry him to the rear to the advanced first-aid post. Here he is attended by a doctor, perhaps assisted by two R. A. M. C. men. Then he is put into a motor ambulance, manned by a crew of two or three. At the field hospital, where he generally goes under an anæsthetic, either to have his wounds cleaned or to be operated on, he requires the services of about three to five persons. From this point another ambulance ride impresses more men in his service, and then at the ambulance train, another corps of doctors, R. A. M. C. men, Red Cross nurses, and the train's crew. From the train he enters the base hospital or Casualty Clearing Station, where a good-sized corps of doctors, nurses, etc., are kept busy. Another ambulance journey is next in order—this time to the hospital ship. He crosses the Channel, arrives in Blighty—more ambulances and perhaps a ride for five hours on an English Red Cross train with its crew of Red Cross workers, and at last he reaches the hospital. Generally he stays from two to six months, or longer, in this hospital. From here he is sent to a convalescent home for six weeks.

If by wounds he is unfitted for further service, he is discharged, given a pension, or committed to a Soldiers' Home for the rest of his life,—and still the expense piles up. When you realize that all the ambulances, trains, and ships, not to mention the man-power, used in transporting a wounded man, could be used for supplies, ammunition, and reinforcements for the troops at the front, it will not appear strange that from a

strictly military standpoint, a dead man is sometimes better than a live one (if wounded).

Not long after the first digging party, our General
decided, after a careful tour of inspection of the
communication trenches, upon *"an ideal spot,"*
as he termed it, for a machine-gun emplacement.
Took his map, made a dot on it, and as he was
wont, wrote "dig here," and the next night we
dug.

There were twenty in the party, myself included.
Armed with picks, shovels, and empty sandbags
we arrived at the "ideal spot" and started digging. The moon was very bright, but we did not
care as we were well out of sight of the German
lines.

We had gotten about three feet down, when the
fellow next to me, after a mighty stroke with his
pick, let go of the handle, and pinched his nose
with his thumb and forefinger, at the same time
letting out the explosion, "Gott strafe me pink,
I'm bloody well gassed, not 'alf I ain't." I
quickly turned in his direction with an inquiring
look, at the same instant reaching for my gas bag.
I soon found out what was ailing him. One whiff
was enough and I lost no time in also pinching
my nose. The stench was awful. The rest of the

digging party dropped their picks and shovels and beat it for the weather side of that solitary pick. The officer came over and inquired why the work had suddenly ceased, holding our noses, we simply pointed in the direction of the smell. He went over to the pick, immediately clapped his hand over his nose, made an "about turn" and came back. Just then our Captain came along and investigated, but after about a minute said we had better carry on with the digging, that he did not see why we should have stopped as the odor was very faint, but if necessary he would allow us to use our gas helmets while digging. He would stay and see the thing through, but he had to report back at Brigade Headquarters immediately. We wished that we were Captains and also had a date at Brigade Headquarters. With our gas helmets on we again attacked that hole and uncovered the decomposed body of a German; the pick was sticking in his chest. One of the men fainted. I was that one. Upon this our Lieutenant halted proceedings and sent word back to headquarters and word came back that after we filled in the hole we could knock off for the night. This was welcome tidings to us, because——

Next day the General changed the dot on his

map and another emplacement was completed
the following night.

The odor from a dug-up, decomposed human
body has an effect which is hard to describe. It
first produces a nauseating feeling, which, especially after eating, causes vomiting. This relieves
you temporarily, but soon a weakening sensation
follows, which leaves you limp as a dish-rag. Your
spirits are at their lowest ebb and you feel a sort
of hopeless helplessness and a mad desire to escape
it all, to get to the open fields and the perfume of
the flowers in Blighty. There is a sharp, prickling
sensation in the nostrils, which reminds one of
breathing coal gas through a radiator in the floor,
and you want to sneeze, but cannot. This was
the effect on me, surmounted by a vague horror
of the awfulness of the thing and an ever-recurring
reflection that, perhaps I, sooner or later, would
be in such a state and be brought to light by the
blow of a pick in the hands of some Tommy on a
digging party.

Several times I have experienced this odor,
but never could get used to it; the enervating sensation was always present. It made me hate
war and wonder why such things were counte-
nanced by civilization, and all the spice and glory

of the conflict would disappear, leaving the grim reality. But after leaving the spot and filling your lungs with deep breaths of pure, fresh air, you forget and once again want to be "up and at them."

CHAPTER XV

LISTENING POST

IT was six in the morning when we arrived at our rest billets, and we were allowed to sleep until noon; that is, if we wanted to go without our breakfast. For sixteen days we remained in rest billets, digging roads, drilling, and other fatigues, and then back into the front-line trench.

Nothing happened that night, but the next afternoon I found out that a bomber is general utility man in a section.

About five o'clock in the afternoon our Lieutenant came down the trench and stopping in front of a bunch of us on the fire step, with a broad grin on his face, asked:

"Who is going to volunteer for listening post to-night? I need two men."

It is needless to say no one volunteered, because it is anything but a cushy job. I began to feel uncomfortable as I knew it was getting around for my turn. Sure enough, with another grin, he said:

"Empey, you and Wheeler are due, so come down into my dugout for instructions at six o'clock."

Just as he left and was going around a traverse, Fritz turned loose with a machine gun and the bullets ripped the sandbags right over his head. It gave me great pleasure to see him duck against the parapet. He was getting a taste of what we would get later out in front.

Then, of course, it began to rain. I knew it was the forerunner of a miserable night for us. Every time I had to go out in front, it just naturally rained. Old Jupiter Pluvius must have had it in for me.

At six we reported for instructions. They were simple and easy. All we had to do was to crawl out into No Man's Land, lie on our bellies with our ears to the ground and listen for the tap tap of the German engineers or sappers who might be tunnelling under No Man's Land to establish a mine-head beneath our trench.

Of course, in our orders we were told not to be captured by German patrols or reconnoitering parties. Lots of breath is wasted on the Western Front giving silly cautions.

As soon as it was dark, Wheeler and I crawled to our post which was about half-way between the lines. It was raining bucketsful, the ground was a sea of sticky mud and clung to us like glue.

We took turns in listening with our ears to the ground. I would listen for twenty minutes while Wheeler would be on the *qui vive* for German patrols.

We each wore a wrist-watch, and believe me, neither one of us did over twenty minutes. The rain soaked us to the skin and our ears were full of mud.

Every few minutes a bullet would crack overhead or a machine gun would traverse back and forth.

Then all firing suddenly ceased. I whispered to Wheeler, "Keep your eye skinned, mate, most likely Fritz has a patrol out,—that's why the Boches have stopped firing."

We were each armed with a rifle and bayonet and three Mills bombs to be used for defense only.

I had my ear to the ground. All of a sudden I heard faint, dull thuds. In a very low, but excited voice, I whispered to Wheeler, "I think they are mining, listen."

He put his ear to the ground and in an unsteady voice spoke into my ear:

"Yank, that's a patrol and it's heading our way. For God's sake keep still."

I was as still as a mouse and was scared stiff.

Hardly breathing and with eyes trying to pierce the inky blackness, we waited. I would have given a thousand pounds to have been safely in my dugout.

Then we plainly heard footsteps and our hearts stood still.

A dark form suddenly loomed up in front of me, it looked as big as the Woolworth Building. I could hear the blood rushing through my veins and it sounded as loud as Niagara Falls.

Forms seemed to emerge from the darkness. There were seven of them in all. I tried to *wish* them away. I never wished harder in my life. They muttered a few words in German and melted into the blackness. I didn't stop wishing either.

All of a sudden we heard a stumble, a muddy splash, and a muttered, "Donner und Blitzen." One of the Boches had tumbled into a shell hole. Neither of us laughed. At that time—it didn't strike us as funny.

About twenty minutes after the Germans had

disappeared, something from the rear grabbed me by the foot. I nearly fainted with fright. Then a welcome whisper in a cockney accent.

"I s'y, myte, we've come to relieve you."

Wheeler and I crawled back to our trench, we looked like wet hens and felt worse. After a swig of rum we were soon fast asleep on the fire step in our wet clothes.

The next morning I was as stiff as a poker and every joint ached like a bad tooth, but I was still alive, so it did not matter.

CHAPTER XVI

BATTERY D 238

THE day after this I received the glad tidings that I would occupy the machine-gunners' dugout right near the advanced artillery observation post. This dugout was a roomy affair, dry as tinder, and *real* cots in it. These cots had been made by the R. E.'s who had previously occupied the dugout. I was the first to enter and promptly made a sign board with my name and number on it and suspended it from the foot of the most comfortable cot therein.

In the trenches, it is always "first come, first served," and this is lived up to by all.

Two R. F. A. men (Royal Field Artillery) from the nearby observation post were allowed the privilege of stopping in this dugout while off duty.

One of these men, Bombadier Wilson by name, who belonged to Battery D 238, seemed to take a liking to me, and I returned this feeling.

In two days' time we were pretty chummy, and he told me how his battery in the early days of the war had put over a stunt on Old Pepper, and had gotten away with it.

I will endeavor to give the story as far as memory will permit in his own words:

"I came out with the First Expeditionary Force, and like all the rest, thought we would have the enemy licked in jig time, and be able to eat Christmas dinner at home. Well, so far, I have eaten two Christmas dinners in the trenches, and am liable to eat two more, the way things are pointing. That is, if Fritz don't drop a 'whizz-bang' on me, and send me to Blighty. Sometimes I wish I would get hit, because it's no great picnic out here, and twenty-two months of it makes you fed up.

"It's fairly cushy now compared to what it used to be, although I admit this trench is a trifle rough. Now, we send over five shells to their one. We are getting our own back, but in the early days it was different. Then you had to take everything without a reply. In fact, we would get twenty shells in return for every one we sent over. Fritz seemed to enjoy it, but we British didn't, we were the sufferers. Just one

casualty after another.   Sometimes whole platoons
would disappear, especially when a 'Jack Johnson'
plunked into their middle.   It got so bad, that a
fellow, when writing home, wouldn't ask for any
cigarettes to be sent out, because he was afraid
he wouldn't be there to receive them.

"After the drive to Paris was turned back,
trench warfare started.   Our General grabbed a
map, drew a pencil line across it, and said, 'Dig
here,' then he went back to his tea, and Tommy
armed himself with a pick and shovel, and started
digging.   He's been digging ever since.

"Of course, we dug those trenches at night,
but it was hot work what with the rifle and
machine-gun fire.   The stretcher-bearers worked
harder than the diggers.

"Those trenches, bloomin' ditches, I call them,
were a nightmare.   They were only about five
feet deep, and you used to get the backache from
bending down.   It wasn't exactly safe to stand
upright either, because as soon as your napper
showed over the top, a bullet would bounce off it,
or else come so close it would make your hair
stand.

"We used to fill sandbags and stick them on top
of the parapet to make it higher, but no use, they

would be there about an hour, and then Fritz would turn loose and blow them to bits. My neck used to be sore from ducking shells and bullets.

"Where my battery was stationed, a hasty trench had been dug, which the boys nicknamed 'Suicide Ditch,' and believe me, Yank, this was the original 'Suicide Ditch.' All the others are imitations.

"When a fellow went into that trench, it was an even gamble that he would come out on a stretcher. At one time, a Scotch battalion held it, and when they heard the betting was even money that they'd come out on stretchers, they grabbed all the bets in sight. Like a lot of bally idiots several of the battery men fell for their game, and put up real money. The 'Jocks' suffered a lot of casualties, and the prospects looked bright for the battery men to collect some easy money. So when the battalion was relieved, the gamblers lined up. Several 'Jocks' got their money for emerging safely, but the ones who clicked it, weren't there to pay. The artillery-men had never thought it out that way. Those Scotties were bound to be sure winners, no matter how the wind blew. So take a tip from me, never bet with a Scottie, 'cause you'll lose money.

"At one part of our trench where a communication trench joined the front line, a Tommy had stuck up a wooden sign-post with three hands or arms on it. One of the hands pointing to the German lines read, 'To Berlin,' the one pointing down the communication trench read, 'To Blighty,' while the other said, 'Suicide Ditch, Change Here for Stretchers.'

"Farther down from this guide post the trench ran through an old orchard. On the edge of this orchard our battery had constructed an advanced observation post. The trees screened it from the enemy airmen and the roof was turfed. It wasn't cushy like ours, no timber or concrete reinforcements, just walls and roof of sandbags. From it, a splendid view of the German lines could be obtained. This post wasn't exactly safe. It was a hot corner, shells plunking all around, and the bullets cutting leaves off the trees. Many a time when relieving the signaler at the 'phone, I had to crawl on my belly like a worm to keep from being hit.

"It was an observation post sure enough. That's all the use it was. Just observe all day, but never a message back for our battery to open up. You see, at this point of the line there were strict orders not to fire a shell, unless specially ordered to do so from Brigade Headquarters. Blime me, if anyone disobeyed that command, our General—yes, it was Old Pepper,—would have courtmartialed the whole Expeditionary Force. Nobody went out of their way to disobey Old Pepper in those days, because he couldn't be called a parson; he was more like a pirate. If at any time the devil should feel lonely, and sigh for a proper mate, Old Pepper would get the first call. Facing the Germans wasn't half bad compared with an interview with that old firebrand.

"If a company or battalion should give way a few yards against a superor force of Boches, Old Pepper would send for the commanding officer. In about half an hour the officer would come back with his face the color of a brick, and in a few hours, what was left of his command, would be holding their original position.

"I have seen an officer, who wouldn't say ' damn ' for a thousand quid, spend five minutes with the old boy, and when he returned, the flow of language from his lips would make a navvy blush for shame.

"What I am going to tell you is how two of us put it over on the old scamp, and got away with

8

it. It was a risky thing, too, because Old Pepper wouldn't have been exactly mild with us if he had got next to the game.

"Me and my mate, a lad named Harry Cassell, a Bombadier in D 238 Battery, or Lance-Corporal, as you call it in the infantry, used to relieve the telephonists. We would do two hours on and four off. I would be on duty in the advanced observation post, while he would be at the other end of the wire in the battery dugout signaling station. We were supposed to send through orders for the battery to fire when ordered to do so by the observation officer in the advanced post. But very few messages were sent. It was only in case of an actual attack that we would get a chance to earn our 'two and six' a day. You see, Old Pepper had issued orders not to fire except when the orders came from him. And with Old Pepper orders is orders, and made to obey.

"The Germans must have known about these orders, for even in the day their transports and troops used to expose themselves as if they were on parade. This sure got up our nose, sitting there day after day, with fine targets in front of us but unable to send over a shell. We heartily cussed Old Pepper, his orders, the government, the people at home, and everything in general. But the Boches didn't mind cussing, and got very careless. Blime me, they were bally insulting. Used to, when using a certain road, throw their caps into the air as a taunt at our helplessness.

"Cassell had been a telegrapher in civil life and joined up when war was declared. As for me, I knew Morse, learned it at the Signaler's School back in 1910. With an officer in the observation post, we could not carry on the kind of conversation that's usual between two mates, so we used the Morse code. To send, one of us would tap the transmitter with his finger nails, and the one on the other end would get it through the receiver. Many an hour was whiled away in this manner passing compliments back and forth.

"In the observation post, the officer used to sit for hours with a powerful pair of field glasses to his eyes. Through a cleverly concealed loophole he would scan the ground behind the German trenches, looking for targets, and finding many. This officer, Captain A—— by name, had a habit of talking out loud to himself. Sometimes he would vent his opinion, same as a common private does when he's wrought up. Once upon a time the Captain had been on Old Pepper's staff, so he could cuss and blind in the most approved style. Got to be sort of a habit with him.

"About six thousand yards from us, behind the German lines, was a road in plain view of our post. For the last three days, Fritz had brought companies of troops down this road in broad daylight. They were never shelled. Whenever this happened, the Captain would froth at the mouth and let out a volume of Old Pepper's religion which used to make me love him.

"Every battery has a range chart on which distinctive landmarks are noted, with the range for each. These landmarks are called targets, and are numbered. On our battery's chart, that road was called 'Target Seventeen, Range 6000, three degrees, thirty minutes left.' D 238 Battery consisted of four '4.5' howitzers, and fired a thirty-five pound H. E. shell. As you know, H. E. means 'high explosive.' I don't like bumming up my own battery, but we had a record in the Division for direct hits, and our boys were just pining away for a chance to exhibit their skill in the eyes of Fritz.

"On the afternoon of the fourth day of Fritz's contemptuous use of the road mentioned, the Captain and I were at our posts as usual. Fritz was *strafeing* us pretty rough, just like he's doing now. The shells were playing leapfrog all through that orchard.

"I was carrying on a conversation in our 'tap' code with Cassell at the other end. It ran something like this:

"'Say, Cassell, how would you like to be in the saloon bar of the King's Arms down Rye Lane with a bottle of Bass in front of you, and that blonde barmaid waiting to fill 'em up again?'

"Cassell had a fancy for that particular blonde. The answer came back in the shape of a volley of cusses. I changed the subject.

"After awhile our talk veered round to the way the Boches had been exposing themselves on the road known on the chart as Target Seventeen. What we said about those Boches would never have passed the Reichstag, though I believe it would have gone through our Censor easily enough.

"The bursting shells were making such a din that I packed up talking and took to watching the Captain. He was fidgeting around on an old sandbag with the glass to his eye. Occasionally he would let out a grunt, and make some remark I couldn't hear on account of the noise, but I guessed what it was all right. Fritz was getting fresh again on that road.

"Cassell had been sending in the 'tap code' to me, but I was fed up and didn't bother with it. Then he sent O. S., and I was all attention, for this was a call used between us which meant that something important was on. I was all ears in an instant. Then Cassell turned loose.

"'You blankety blank dud, I have been trying to raise you for fifteen minutes. What's the matter, are you asleep?' (Just as if anyone could have slept in that infernal racket!) 'Never mind framing a nasty answer. Just listen.'

"'Are you game for putting something over on the Boches, and Old Pepper all in one?'

"I answered that I was game enough when it came to putting it over the Boches, but confessed that I had a weakening of the spine, even at the mention of Old Pepper's name.

"He came back with, 'It's so absurdly easy and simple that there is no chance of the old heathen rumbling it. Anyway, if we're caught, I'll take the blame.'

"Under those conditions I told him to spit out his scheme. It was so daring and simple that it took my breath away. This is what he proposed:

"If the Boches should use that road again, to send by the tap system the target and range. I had previously told him about our Captain talking out loud as if he were sending through orders. Well, if this happened, I was to send the dope to Cassell and he would transmit it to the Battery Commander as officially coming through the observation post. Then the battery would open up. Afterwards, during the investigation, Cassell would swear he received it direct. They would have to believe him, because it was impossible from his post in the battery dugout to know that the road was being used at that time by the Germans. And also it was impossible for him to give the target, range, and degrees. You know a battery chart is not passed around among the men like a newspaper from Blighty. From him, the investigation would go to the observation post, and the observing officer could truthfully swear that I had not sent the message by 'phone, and that no orders to fire had been issued by him. The investigators would then be up in the air, we would be safe, the Boches would receive a good bashing, and we would get our own back on Old Pepper. It was too good to be true. I gleefully fell in with the scheme, and told Cassell I was his meat.

"Then I waited with beating heart, and watched the Captain like a hawk.

"He was beginning to fidget again and was drumming on the sandbags with his feet. At last, turning to me, he said:

"'Wilson, this army is a blankety blank washout. What's the use of having artillery if it is not allowed to fire? The government at home ought to be hanged with some of their red tape. It's through them that we have no shells.'

"I answered, 'Yes sir,' and started sending this opinion over the wire to Cassell, but the Captain interrupted me with:

"'Keep those infernal fingers still. What's the matter, getting the nerves? When I'm talking to you, pay attention.'

"My heart sank. Supposing he had rumbled that tapping, then all would be up with our plan. I stopped drumming with my fingers, and said:

"'Beg your pardon, sir, just a habit with me.'

"'And a damned silly one, too,' he answered, turning to his glasses again, and I knew I was safe. He had not tumbled to the meaning of that tapping.

"All at once, without turning round, he exclaimed:

"'Well, of all the nerve I've ever run across, this takes the cake. Those — — Boches are using that road again. Blind my eyes, this time it is a whole Brigade of them, transports and all. What a pretty target for our '4.5's.' The beggars know we wont fire. A damned shame I call it. Oh, just for a chance to turn D 238 loose on them.'

"I was trembling with excitement. From repeated stolen glances at the Captain's range chart, that road with its range was burned into my mind.

"Over the wire I tapped, 'D 238 Battery, Target Seventeen, Range 6000, three degrees, thirty minutes, left, Salvo, Fire.' Cassell O. K.'d my message, and with the receiver pressed against my ear, I waited and listened. In a couple of minutes very faintly over the wire came the voice of our Battery Commander issuing the order: 'D 238 Battery. Salvo! Fire!'

"Then a roar through the receiver as the four guns belched forth, a screaming and whistling overhead, and the shells were on their way.

"The Captain jumped as if he were shot, and let out a great big expressive Damn, and eagerly turned his glasses in the direction of the German road. I also strained my eyes watching that target. Four black clouds of dust rose up right in the middle of the German column. Four direct hits—another record for D 238.

"The shells kept on whistling overhead, and I had counted twenty-four of them when the firing suddenly ceased. When the smoke and dust clouds lifted, the destruction on that road was awful. Overturned limbers and guns, wagons smashed up, troops fleeing in all directions. The road and roadside were spotted all over with little field gray dots, the toll of our guns.

"The Captain, in his excitement, had slipped off the sandbag, and was on his knees in the mud, the glass still at his eye. He was muttering to himself and slapping his thigh with his disengaged hand. At every slap a big round juicy cuss word would escape from his lips followed by:

"'Good, Fine,—Marvelous, Pretty Work, Direct Hits, All.'

"Then he turned to me and shouted:

"'Wilson, what do you think of it? Did you ever see the like of it in your life? Damn fine work, I call it.'

"Pretty soon a look of wonder stole over his face, and he exclaimed:

"'But who in hell gave them the order to fire. Range and everything correct, too. I know I didn't. Wilson, did I give you any order for the Battery to open up? Of course, I didn't, did I?'

"I answered very emphatically, 'No, sir, you gave no command. Nothing went through this post. I am absolutely certain on that point, sir.'

"'Of course nothing went through,' he replied. Then his face fell, and he muttered out loud:

"'But, by Jove, wait till Old Pepper gets wind of this. There'll be fur flying.'

"Just then Bombadier Cassell cut in on the wire:

"'General's compliments to Captain A——. He directs that officer and signaler report at the double to Brigade Headquarters as soon as relieved. Relief is now on the way.'

"In an undertone to me, 'Keep a brass front, Wilson, and for God's sake, stick.' I answered with, 'Rely on me, mate,' but I was trembling all over.

"I gave the General's message to the Captain, and started packing up.

"The relief arrived, and as we left the post the Captain said:

"'Now for the fireworks, and I know they'll be good and plenty.' They were.

"When we arrived at the gun pits, the Battery Commander, the Sergeant-Major, and Cassell were waiting for us. We fell in line and the funeral march to Brigade Headquarters started.

"Arriving at Headquarters the Battery Commander was the first to be interviewed. This was behind closed doors. From the roaring and explosions of Old Pepper it sounded as if raw meat was being thrown to the lions. Cassell, later, described it as sounding like a bombing raid. In about two minutes the officer reappeared. The sweat was pouring from his forehead, and his face was the color of a beet. He was speechless. As he passed the Captain he jerked his thumb in the direction of the lion's den and went out. Then the Captain went in, and the lions were once again fed. The Captain stayed about twenty minutes and came out. I couldn't see his face, but the droop in his shoulders was enough. He looked like a wet hen.

"The door of the General's room opened, and Old Pepper stood in the doorway. With a roar he shouted:

"'Which one of you is Cassell? Damn me, get your heels together when I speak! Come in here!'

"Cassell started to say, 'Yes, sir.'

"But Old Pepper roared, 'Shut up!'

"Cassell came out in five minutes. He said nothing, but as he passed me, he put his tongue into his cheek and winked, then turning to the closed door, he stuck his thumb to his nose and left.

"Then the Sergeant-Major's turn came. He didn't come out our way. Judging by the roaring, Old Pepper must have eaten him.

"When the door opened, and the General beckoned to me, my knees started to play *Home, Sweet Home* against each other.

"My interview was very short.

"Old Pepper glared at me when I entered, and then let loose.

"'Of course you don't know anything about it. You're just like the rest. Ought to have a nursing bottle around your neck, and a nipple in your teeth. Soldiers, by gad, you turn my stomach to look at you. Win this war, when England sends out such samples as I have in my Brigade! Not likely! Now, sir, tell me what you *don't* know about this affair. Speak up, out with it. Don't be gaping at me like a fish. Spit it out.'

"I stammered, 'Sir, I know absolutely nothing.'

"'That's easy to see,' he roared; 'that stupid face tells me that. Shut up. Get out; but I think you are a damned liar just the same. Back to your battery.'

"I saluted and made my exit.

"That night the Captain sent for us. With fear and trembling we went to his dugout. He was alone. After saluting, we stood at attention in front of him and waited. His say was short.

"'Don't you two ever get it into your heads that Morse is a dead language. I've known it for years. The two of you had better get rid of that nervous habit of tapping transmitters; it's dangerous. That's all.'

"We saluted, and were just going out the door of the dugout when the Captain called us back, and said:

"'Smoke Goldflakes? Yes? Well there are two tins of them on my table. Go back to the battery, and keep your tongues between your teeth. Understand?'

"We understood.

"For five weeks afterwards our battery did nothing but extra fatigues. We were satisfied and so were the men. It was worth it to put one over on Old Pepper, to say nothing of the injury caused to Fritz's feelings."

When Wilson had finished his story I looked up, and the dugout was jammed. An artillery Captain and two officers had also entered and stayed for the finish. Wilson spat out an enormous quid of tobacco, looked up, saw the Captain, and got as red as a carnation. The Captain smiled and left. Wilson whispered to me:

"Blime me, Yank, I see where I click for crucifixion. That Captain is the same one that chucked us the Goldflakes in his dugout and here I have been 'chucking me weight about in his hearing.'"

Wilson never clicked his crucifixion.

Quite a contrast to Wilson was another character in our Brigade named Scott, we called him "Old Scotty" on account of his age. He was fifty-seven, although looking forty. "Old Scotty" had been born in the Northwest and had served with the Northwest Mounted Police. He was a typical cow-puncher and Indian fighter and was a dead shot with the rifle, and took no pains to disguise this fact from us. He used to take care of his rifle as if it were a baby. In his spare moments you could always see him cleaning it or polishing the stock. Woe betide the man, who by mistake, happened to get hold of this rifle; he soon found out his error. Scott was as deaf as a mule, and it was amusing at parade to watch him in the manual of arms, slyly glancing out of the corner of his eye at the man next to him to see what the order was. How he passed the doctor was a mystery to us, he must have bluffed his way through, because he certainly was independent. Beside him the Fourth of July looked like Good Friday. He wore at the time a large sombrero, had a Mexican stock saddle over his shoulder, a lariat on his arm, and a "forty-five" hanging from his hip. Dumping this paraphernalia on the floor he went up to the recruiting officer and shouted: "I'm from America, west of the Rockies, and want to join your damned army. I've got no use for a German and can shoot some. At Scotland Yard they turned me down; said I was deaf and so I am. I don't hanker to ship in with a damned mud crunching outfit, but the cavalry's full, so I guess this regiment's better than none, so trot out your papers and I'll sign 'em." He told them he was forty and slipped by. I was on recruiting service at the time he applied for enlistment.

It was Old Scotty's great ambition to be a

sniper or "body snatcher" as Mr. Atkins calls it. The day that he was detailed as Brigade Sniper, he celebrated his appointment by blowing the whole platoon to fags.

Being a Yank, Old Scotty took a liking to me and used to spin some great yarns about the plains, and the whole platoon would drink these in and ask for more. Ananias was a rookie compared with him.

The ex-plainsman and discipline could not agree, but the officers all liked him, even if he was hard to manage, so when he was detailed as a sniper, a sigh of relief went up from the officers' mess.

Old Scotty had the freedom of the Brigade. He used to draw two or three days' rations and disappear with his glass, range finder, and rifle, and we would see or hear no more of him, until suddenly he would reappear with a couple of notches added to those already on the butt of his rifle. Every time he got a German it meant another notch. He was proud of these notches.

But after a few months Father Rheumatism got him and he was sent to Blighty; the air in the wake of his stretcher was blue with curses. Old Scotty surely could swear; some of his outbursts actually burned you.

9

No doubt, at this writing he is "somewhere in Blighty" pussy footing it on a bridge or along the wall of some munition plant with the "G. R." or Home Defence Corps.

CHAPTER XVII

OUT IN FRONT

AFTER tea, Lieutenant Stores of our section came into the dugout and informed me that I was "for" a reconnoitering patrol and would carry six Mills bombs.

At 11.30 that night twelve men, our Lieutenant, and myself went out in front on a patrol in No Man's Land.

We cruised around in the dark for about two hours, just knocking about looking for trouble, on the lookout for Boche working parties to see what they were doing.

Around two in the morning we were carefully picking our way, about thirty yards in front of the German barbed wire, when we walked into a Boche covering party nearly thirty strong. Then the music started, the fiddler rendered his bill, and we paid.

Fighting in the dark with a bayonet is not very

pleasant. The Germans took it on the run, but our officer was no novice at the game and didn't follow them. He gave the order "down on the ground, hug it close."

Just in time, too, because a volley skimmed over our heads. Then in low tones we were told to separate and crawl back to our trenches, each man on his own.

We could see the flashes of their rifles in the darkness, but the bullets were going over our heads.

We lost three men killed and one wounded in the arm. If it hadn't been for our officers' quick thinking the whole patrol would have probably been wiped out.

After about twenty minutes' wait we went out again and discovered that the Germans had a wiring party working on their barbed wire. We returned to our trenches unobserved with the information and our machine guns immediately got busy.

The next night four men were sent out to go over and examine the German barbed wire and see if they had cut lanes through it; if so, this presaged an early morning attack on our trenches.

Of course, I had to be one of the four selected

for the job. It was just like sending a fellow to
the undertaker's to order his own coffin.

At ten o'clock we started out, armed with
three bombs, a bayonet, and revolver. After
getting into No Man's Land we separated. Crawling four or five feet at a time, ducking star shells,
with strays cracking over head, I reached their
wire. I scouted along this inch by inch, scarcely
breathing. I could hear them talking in their
trench, my heart was pounding against my ribs.
One false move or the least noise from me meant
discovery and almost certain death.

After covering my sector I quietly crawled
back. I had gotten about half-way, when I
noticed that my revolver was missing. It was
pitch dark. I turned about to see if I could find
it; it couldn't be far away, because about three or
four minutes previously I had felt the butt in the
holster. I crawled around in circles and at last
found it, then started on my way back to our
trenches, as I thought.

Pretty soon I reached barbed wire, and was just
going to give the password, when something told
me not to. I put out my hand and touched one of
the barbed wire stakes. It was iron. The British
are of wood, while the German are iron. My

heart stopped beating; by mistake I had crawled back to the German lines.

I turned slowly about and my tunic caught on the wire and made a loud ripping noise.

A sharp challenge rang out. I sprang to my feet, ducking low, and ran madly back toward our lines. The Germans started firing. The bullets were biting all around me, when bang! I ran smash into our wire, and a sharp challenge "'Alt, who comes there?" rang out. I gasped out the password and groping my way through the lane in the wire, tearing my hands and uniform, I tumbled into our trench and was safe, but I was a nervous wreck for an hour, until a drink of rum brought me round.

CHAPTER XVIII

STAGED UNDER FIRE

THREE days after the incident just related our Company was relieved from the front line and carried out. We stayed in reserve billets for about two weeks when we received the welcome news that our division would go back of the line "to rest billets." We would remain in these billets for at least two months, this in order to be restored to our full strength by drafts of recruits from Blighty.

Everyone was happy and contented at these tidings; all you could hear around the billets was whistling and singing. The day after the receipt of the order we hiked for five days, making an average of about twelve kilos per day until we arrived at the small town of O'——.

It took us about three days to get settled and from then on our cushy time started. We would parade from 8.45 in the morning until 12 noon.

Then except for an occasional billet or brigade guard we were on our own. For the first four or five afternoons I spent my time in bringing up to date my neglected correspondence.

Tommy loves to be amused, and being a Yank, they turned to me for something new in this line. I taught them how to pitch horseshoes, and this game made a great hit for about ten days. Then Tommy turned to America for a new diversion. I was up in the air until a happy thought came to me. Why not write a sketch and break Tommy in as an actor?

One evening after "Lights out," when you are not supposed to talk, I imparted my scheme in whispers to the section. They eagerly accepted the idea of forming a Stock Company and could hardly wait until the morning for further details.

After parade, the next afternoon I was almost mobbed. Everyone in the section wanted a part in the proposed sketch. When I informed them that it would take at least ten days of hard work to write the plot, they were bitterly disappointed. I immediately got busy, made a desk out of biscuit tins in the corner of the billet, and put up a sign "Empey & Wallace Theatrical Co." About twenty of the section, upon reading this sign, immediately applied for the position of office boy. I accepted the twenty applicants, and sent them on scouting parties throughout the deserted French village. These parties were to search all the attics for discarded civilian clothes, and anything that we could use in the props of our proposed Company.

About five that night they returned covered with grime and dust, but loaded down with a miscellaneous assortment of everything under the sun. They must have thought that I was going to start a department store, judging from the different things they brought back from their pillage.

After eight days' constant writing I completed a two-act farce comedy which I called *The Diamond Palace Saloon*. Upon the suggestion of one of the boys in the section I sent a proof of the program to a printing house in London. Then I assigned the different parts and started rehearsing. David Belasco would have thrown up his hands in despair at the material which I had to use. Just imagine trying to teach a Tommy, with a strong cockney accent, to impersonate a Bowery Tough or a Southern Negro.

Adjacent to our billet was an open field. We got busy at one end of it and constructed a stage. We secured the lumber for the stage by demolishing an old wooden shack in the rear of our billet.

The first scene was supposed to represent a street on the Bowery in New York. While the scene of the second act was the interior of the Diamond Palace Saloon, also on the Bowery.

In the play I took the part of Abe Switch, a farmer, who had come from Pumpkinville Center, Tennessee, to make his first visit to New York.

In the first scene Abe Switch meets the proprietor of the Diamond Palace Saloon, a ramshackle affair which to the owner was a financial loss.

The proprietor's name was Tom Twistem, his bartender being named Fillem Up.

After meeting Abe, Tom and Fillem Up persuaded him to buy the place, praising it to the skies and telling wondrous tales of the money taken over the bar.

While they are talking, an old Jew named Ikey Cohenstein comes along, and Abe engages him for cashier. After engaging Ikey they meet an old Southern Negro called Sambo, and upon the suggestion of Ikey he is engaged as porter. Then the three of them, arm in arm, leave to take possession of this wonderful palace which Abe had just paid $6,000 for. (Curtain.)

The

KING GEORGE V.
THEATRE

(Erected 1916)

Situated Corner of Sand Bag Terrace and
Ammo Street.

Under Management of Empey and Wallace.

NOTE.—The Management warns all patrons of this
Theatre that they will not be responsible for
injuries received from the unauthorized entrance
of stray shells, "whizz-bangs," or rifle bullets.

Programmes Printed by Everett.

Executive Staff.

A. G. Empey	...	...		*Producer and Playwright*
Jack Wallace	...	...	...	... *Manager*
Richard Turpin	...	...	...	... *Cashier*
George Parsons	...	...	...	... *Stage Manager*
Frederick Houghton		...	...	... *Property Man*
William Everett	....	...	...	... *Electrician*
William Guilford	...	...	...	... *Carpenter*
Sydney Impey	...	...	...	... *Booking Office*
John Foxcroft	...	...	...	... *Head Usher*

NOTE.

The Management requests that patrons will remove their steel helmets.

In case of an attack, keep your seats, don't interrupt the performance

If you don't like the show, leave, don't put on your gas helmets.

Patrons will not bring live bombs into this theatre.

No one allowed past the barbed wire in front of the footlights as it is the actors' only protection. No firing at actors.

It is earnestly requested that any incivility or inattention towards patrons from the employees of this Theatre be reported at the Booking Office, so that the offender may be shot at sunrise (if he gets up in time). ,

Ladies Room in rear of first balcony. Matron in attendance.

Lounging and Smoking Room for gentlemen in the shell-proof cellar. Identification disc must be shown to prove you are a gentleman.

Gentlemen are requested not to swear aloud at actors, the show, playwright or orchestra. It is not their fault that they are rotten, they know it as well as you do.

No tins of Bully Beef or Maconochie Rations accepted at the Booking Office in payment for tickets.

Caste of Characters

(as they appear).

TOM TWISTEM (gang leader and wise guy, owner and proprietor of the Diamond Palace Saloon, out for the dough) ... JACK WALLACE

FILLEM UP (bar tender of the Diamond Palace Saloon, an ex-burglar, a ticket-of-leave man) ... ... WILFRED ISOM

SAMBO (a negro from Virginia, always broke and hungry, joined a minstrel show which went broke and left him stranded in New York) ... ... EDWARD FITZGERALD

IKEY COHENSTEIN (an East Side Jew, New York City, Dealer in Second-hand Clothes and a Moneylender) CHARLES HONNEY

ABE SWITCH (a Farmer, Postmaster, Constable, and owner of the only shop in Pumpkinville Center, Tennessee, U.S.A. First trip to New York City. Left his wife, Miranda, at home) A. G. EMPEY

WEARY WILLIE (a bum, never works and always drunk) A. G. HALL

SID COCAINE (a morphine fiend, a man of few words)
WILLIAM YERRELL

"KID" PAPES (a tough newsboy) ... CHARLES DALTON

"BROADWAY" KATE (Tom Twistem's lady friend, clever at getting the dough) ... ... MADAME ZARA

SING LEE SUNG (a Chinese Laundryman) WILLIAM YERRELL

ALKALI IKE (a Texas Cowboy from the Bad Lands, Texas, expert revolver shot, quick on the draw and shoots from the hip)
A. G. HALL

CUSTOMERS, SOLDIERS, ETC.

Messrs. EMPEY and WALLACE

PRESENT

The Rip Roaring, Side Splitting, Farce Comedy

ENTITLED

The Diamond Palace Saloon

A TRAVESTY ON NEW YORK LIFE,

Acted by the All-Star Caste of the

167th BRIGADE MACHINE GUN COMPANY (Suicide Club)

Section No. 1.

*Written, rehearsed and produced under fire during
the European War, France, 1916.*

~~~~~~~~

Act I.

SCENE I.   Street Scene on the Bowery, New York City.

TIME.   Any old time.

NOTE.   Five minutes interval to enable actors to get a drink.

Act II.

SCENE I. (*one scene is sufficient*) Interior of Diamond Palace Saloon
corner of 3rd Avenue and 12th Street, New York City.

TIME,   Same day as Act I.

~~~~~~~~

Musical Programme

— *Rendered by the Trench Orchestra.* —

I. A. M. ROTTEN   ...   Leader.

Overture	...	...	...	...	...	...	"Hymn of Hate
Selection	...	...	...	...	" How we Love der Kaiser
Intermezzo	...	...	...	...	...	"Stick it into a Hun
March	...	...	...	...	...	...	"On to Berlin
Selection	...	...	...	...	...	...	"Poison Gas

— GOD SAVE THE KING. —

FINIS.

In the second act the curtain rises on the interior of the Diamond Palace Saloon, and the audience gets its first shock. The saloon looks like a pig-pen, two tramps lying drunk on the floor, and the bartender in a dirty shirt with his sleeves rolled up, asleep with his head on the bar.

Enter Abe, Sambo, and Ikey, and the fun commences.

One of the characters in the second act was named Broadway Kate, and I had an awful job to break in one of the Tommies to act and talk like a woman.

Another character was Alkali Ike, an Arizona cow-boy, who just before the close of the play comes into the saloon and wrecks it with his revolver.

We had eleven three-hour rehearsals before I thought it advisable to present the sketch to the public.

The whole Brigade was crazy to witness the first performance. This performance was scheduled for Friday night and everyone was full of anticipation when bang! orders came through that the Brigade would move at two that afternoon. Cursing and blinding was the order of things upon the receipt of this order, but we moved.

That night we reached the little village of S——
and again went into rest billets. We were to be
there two weeks. Our Company immediately got
busy and scoured the village for a suitable place
in which to present our production. Then we
received another shock.

A rival company was already established in the
village. They called themselves "The Bow
Bells," and put on a sketch entitled *Blighty—What
Hopes?* They were the Divisional Concert
Party.

We hoped they all would be soon in Blighty to
give us a chance.

This company charged an admission of a franc
per head, and that night our company went *en
masse* to see their performance. It really was
good.

I had a sinking sensation when I thought of
running my sketch in opposition to it.

In one of their scenes they had a soubrette called
Flossie. The soldier that took this part was clever
and made a fine appearing and chic girl. We
immediately fell in love with her until two days
after, while we were on a march, we passed Flossie
with *her* sleeves rolled up and the sweat pouring
from *her* face unloading shells from a motor lorry.

As our section passed her I yelled out: "Hello, Flossie, Blighty—What Hopes?" Her reply made our love die out instantly.

"Ah, go to hell!"

This brought quite a laugh from the marching column directed at me, and I instantly made up my mind that our sketch should immediately run in opposition to *Blighty—What Hopes?*

When we returned to our billet from the march, Curley Wallace, my theatrical partner, came running over to me and said he had found a swanky place in which to produce our show.

After taking off my equipment, and followed by the rest of the section, I went over to the building he had picked out. It was a monstrous barn with a platform at one end which would make an ideal stage. The section got right on the job, and before night had that place rigged out in apple-pie order.

The next day was Sunday and after church parade we put all our time on a dress rehearsal, and it went fine.

I made four or five large signs announcing that our company would open up that evening at the King George the Fifth Theatre, on the corner of Ammo Street and Sandbag Terrace. General admission was one half franc. First ten rows in or-

chestra one franc, and boxes two francs. By this
time our printed programs had returned from
London, and I further announced that on the night
of the first performance a program would be given
free of charge to men holding tickets costing a
franc or over.

We had an orchestra of seven men and seven
different instruments. This orchestra was excellent, while they were not playing.

The performance was scheduled to start at 6 P.M.

At 5.15 there was a mob in front of our one
entrance and it looked like a big night. We had
two boxes each accommodating four people, and
these we immediately sold out. Then a brilliant
idea came to Ikey Cohenstein. Why not use the
rafters overhead, call them boxes, and charge two
francs for a seat on them? The only difficulty was
how were the men to reach these boxes, but to
Ikey this was a mere detail.

He got long ropes and tied one end around each
rafter and then tied a lot of knots in the ropes.
These ropes would take the place of stairways.

We figured out that the rafters would seat about
forty men and sold that number of tickets accordingly.

When the ticket-holders for the boxes got a

glimpse of the rafters and were informed that they had to use the rope stairway, there was a howl of indignation, but we had their money and told them that if they did not like it they could write to the management later and their money would be refunded; but under these conditions they would not be allowed to witness the performance that night.

After a little grousing they accepted the situation with the promise that if the show was rotten they certainly would let us know about it during the performance.

Everything went lovely and it was a howling success, until Alkali Ike appeared on the scene with his revolver loaded with blank cartridges. Behind the bar on a shelf was a long line of bottles. Alkali Ike was supposed to start on the left of this line and break six of the bottles by firing at them with his revolver. Behind these bottles a piece of painted canvas was supposed to represent the back of the bar, at each shot from Alkali's pistol a man behind the scenes would hit one of the bottles with his entrenching tool handle and smash it, to give the impression that Alkali was a good shot.

Alkali Ike started in and aimed at the right of the line of bottles instead of the left, and the poor

boob behind the scenes started breaking the bottles
on the left, and then the box-holders turned loose;
but outside of this little fiasco the performance was
a huge success, and we decided to run it for a week.

New troops were constantly coming through,
and for six performances we had the "S. R. O."
sign suspended outside.

CHAPTER XIX

ON HIS OWN

OF course Tommy cannot always be producing plays under fire but while in rest billets he has numerous other ways of amusing himself. He is a great gambler, but never plays for large stakes. Generally, in each Company, you will find a regular Canfield. This man banks nearly all the games of chance and is an undisputed authority on the rules of gambling. Whenever there is an argument among the Tommies about some uncertain point as to whether Houghton is entitled to Watkins' sixpence, the matter is taken to the recognized authority and his decision is final.

The two most popular games are "Crown and Anchor" and "House."

The paraphernalia used in "Crown and Anchor" consists of a piece of canvas two feet by three feet. This is divided into six equal squares. In these squares are painted a club, diamond, heart, spade, crown, and an anchor, one device to a square.

There are three dice used, each dice marked the same as the canvas. The banker sets up his gambling outfit in the corner of a billet and starts ballyhooing until a crowd of Tommies gather around; then the game starts.

The Tommies place bets on the squares, the crown or anchor being played the most. The banker then rolls his three dice and collects or pays out as the case may be. If you play the crown and one shows up on the dice, you get even money, if two show up, you receive two to one, and if three, three to one. If the crown does not appear and you have bet on it, you lose, and so on. The percentage for the banker is large if every square is played, but if the crowd is partial to, say two squares, he has to trust to luck. The banker generally wins.

The game of "House" is very popular also. It takes two men to run it. This game consists of numerous squares of cardboard containing three rows of numbers, five numbers to a row. The numbers run from one to ninety. Each card has a different combination.

The French *estaminets* in the villages are open from eleven in the morning until one in the afternoon in accordance with army orders.

After dinner the Tommies congregate at these places to drink French beer at a penny a glass and play "House."

As soon as the *estaminet* is sufficiently crowded the proprietors of the "House Game" get busy and as they term it "form a school." This consists of going around and selling cards at a franc each. If they have ten in the school, the backers of the game deduct two francs for their trouble and the winner gets eight francs.

Then the game starts. Each buyer places his card before him on the table, first breaking up matches into fifteen pieces

One of the backers of the game has a small cloth bag in which are ninety cardboard squares, each with a number printed thereon, from one to ninety. He raps on the table and cries out, "Eyes down, my lucky lads."

All noise ceases and everyone is attention.

The croupier places his hand in the bag and draws forth a numbered square and immediately calls out the number. The man who owns the card with that particular number on it, covers the square with a match. The one who covers the fifteen numbers on his card first shouts "House." The other backer immediately comes over to him and verifies the card, by calling out the numbers thereon to the man with the bag. As each number is called he picks it out of the ones picked from the bag and says, "Right." If the count is right he shouts, "House correct, pay the lucky gentleman, and sell him a card for the next school." The "lucky gentleman" generally buys one unless he has a Semitic trace in his veins.

Then another collection is made, a school formed, and they carry on with the game.

The caller-out has many nicknames for the numbers such as "Kelly's Eye" for one, "Leg's Eleven" for eleven, "Clickety-click" for sixty-six, or "Top of the house" meaning ninety.

The game is honest and quite enjoyable. Sometimes you have fourteen numbers on your card covered and you are waiting for the fifteenth to be called. In an imploring voice you call out, "Come on, Watkins, chum, I'm sweating on 'Kelly's Eye.'"

Watkins generally replies, "Well keep out of a draught, you'll catch cold."

Another game is "Pontoon" played with cards; it is the same as our "Black Jack," or "Twenty-one."

A card game called "Brag" is also popular.

Using a casino deck, the dealer deals each player three cards. It is similar to our poker, except for the fact that you only use three cards and cannot draw. The deck is never shuffled until a man shows three of a kind or a "prile" as it is called. The value of the hands are, high card, a pair, a run, a flush or three of a kind or "prile." The limit is generally a penny, so it is hard to win a fortune.

The next in popularity is a card game called "Nap." It is well named. Every time I played it I went to sleep.

Whist and Solo Whist are played by the high-brows of the Company.

When the gamblers tire of all other games they try "Banker and Broker."

I spent a week trying to teach some of the Tommies how to play poker, but because I won thirty-five francs they declared that they didn't "Fawncy" the game.

Tommy plays few card games; the general run never heard of poker, euchre, seven up, or pinochle. They have a game similar to pinochle called "Royal Bezique," but few know how to play it.

Generally there are two decks of cards in a section, and in a short time they are so dog-eared and greasy, you can hardly tell the ace of spades from the ace of hearts. The owners of these decks sometimes condescend to lend them after much coaxing.

So you see, Mr. Atkins has his fun mixed in with his hardships, and, contrary to popular belief, the rank and file of the British Army in the trenches is one big happy family. Now in Virginia, at school, I was fed on old McGuffy's primary reader, which gave me an opinion of an Englishman about equal to a '76 Minute Man's backed up by a Sinn Feiner's. But I found Tommy to be the best of mates and a gentleman through and through. He never thinks of knocking his officers. If one makes a costly mistake and Tommy pays with his blood, there is no general condemnation of the officer. He is just pitied. It is exactly the same as it was with the Light Brigade at Balaclava, to say nothing of Gallipoli, Neuve Chapelle, and Loos. Personally I remember a little incident where twenty of us were sent on a trench raid, only two of us returning, but I will tell this story later on.

I said it was a big happy family, and so it is, but as in all happy families, there are servants, so in the British Army there are also servants, officers' servants, or "O. S." as they are termed. In the American Army the common name for them is

Right Arm Smashed by Shell (in Plaster Cast); has been Told it
will Have to be Amputated.

Photo taken just after the doctor had informed him that he would lose his arm.
"Lamp the grin!"
Another captured Prussian helmet on his head.   We have many.

"dog robbers." From a controversy in the English papers, Winston Churchill made the statement, as far as I can remember, that the officers' servants in the British forces totaled nearly two hundred thousand. He claimed that this removed two hundred thousand exceptionally good and well-trained fighters from the actual firing line, claiming that the officers, when selecting a man for servant's duty, generally picked the man who had been out the longest and knew the ropes.

But from my observation I find that a large percentage of the servants do go over the top, but behind the lines, they very seldom engage in digging parties, fatigues, parades, or drills. This work is as necessary as actually engaging in an attack, therefore I think that it would be safe to say that the all-round work of the two hundred thousand is about equal to fifty thousand men who are on straight military duties. In numerous instances, officers' servants hold the rank of lance-corporals and they assume the same duties and authority of a butler. The one stripe giving him precedence over the other servants.

There are lots of amusing stories told of "O. S."

One day one of our majors went into the servants' billet and commenced "blinding" at them, saying that his horse had no straw, and that he personally knew that straw had been issued for this purpose. He called the lance-corporal to account. The Corporal answered, "Blime me, sir, the straw was issued, but there wasn't enough left over from the servants' beds; in fact, we had to use some of the 'ay to 'elp out, sir."

It is needless to say that the servants dispensed with their soft beds that particular night.

Nevertheless it is not the fault of the individual officer, it is just the survival of a quaint old English custom. You know an Englishman cannot be changed in a day.

But the average English officer is a good sport, he will sit on a fire step and listen respectfully to Private Jones's theory of the way the war should be conducted. This war is gradually crumbling the once unsurmountable wall of caste.

You would be convinced of this if you could see King George go among his men on an inspecting tour under fire, or pause before a little wooden cross in some shell-tossed field with tears in his eyes as he reads the inscription. And a little later perhaps bend over a wounded man on a stretcher, patting him on the head.

More than once in a hospital I have seen a

titled Red Cross nurse fetching and carrying for a wounded soldier, perhaps the one who in civil life delivered the coal at her back door. To-day she does not shrink from lighting his fag or even washing his grimy body.

Tommy admires Albert of Belgium because he is not a pusher of men, he LEADS them. With him it's not a case of "take that trench," it is "come on and we will take it."

It is amusing to notice the different characteristics of the Irish, Scotch, and English soldiers. The Irish and Scotch are very impetuous, especially when it comes to bayonet fighting, while the Englishman, though a trifle slower, thoroughly does his bit; he is more methodical and has the grip of a bulldog on a captured position. He is slower to think, that is the reason why he never knows when he is licked.

Twenty minutes before going over the top the English Tommy will sit on the fire step and thoroughly examine the mechanism of his rifle to see that it is in working order and will fire properly. After this examination he is satisfied and ready to meet the Boches.

But the Irishman or Scotchman sits on the fire step, his rifle with bayonet fixed between his knees,

the butt of which perhaps is sinking into the mud,
—the bolt couldn't be opened with a team of horses
it is so rusty,—but he spits on his sleeve and slowly
polishes his bayonet; when this is done he also is
ready to argue with Fritz.

It is not necessary to mention the Colonials
(the Canadians, Australians, and New Zealanders),
the whole world knows what they have done for
England.

The Australian and New Zealander is termed the
"Anzac," taking the name from the first letters
of their official designation, Australian and New
Zealand Army Corps.

Tommy divides the German army into three
classes according to their fighting abilities. They
rank as follows, Prussians, Bavarians, and Saxons.

When up against a Prussian regiment it is a
case of keep your napper below the parapet and
duck. A bang-bang all the time and a war is on.
The Bavarians are little better, but the Saxons are
fairly good sports and are willing occasionally to
behave as gentlemen and take it easy, but you
cannot trust any of them overlong.

At one point of the line the trenches were about
thirty-two yards apart. This sounds horrible,
but in fact it was easy, because neither side could

shell the enemy's front-line trench for fear shells would drop into their own. This eliminated artillery fire.

In these trenches when up against the Prussians and Bavarians, Tommy had a hot time of it, but when the Saxons "took over" it was a picnic, they would yell across that they were Saxons and would not fire. Both sides would sit on the parapet and carry on a conversation. This generally consisted of Tommy telling them how much he loved the Kaiser while the Saxons informed Tommy that King George was a particular friend of theirs and hoped that he was doing nicely.

When the Saxons were to be relieved by Prussians or Bavarians, they would yell this information across No Man's Land and Tommy would immediately tumble into his trench and keep his head down.

If an English regiment was to be relieved by the wild Irish, Tommy would tell the Saxons, and immediately a volley of "Donner und Blitzen's" could be heard, and it was Fritz's turn to get a crick in his back from stooping, and the people in Berlin would close their windows.

Usually when an Irishman takes over a trench, just before "stand down" in the morning, he sticks his rifle over the top aimed in the direction of Berlin and engages in what is known as the "mad minute." This consists of firing fifteen shots in a minute. He is not aiming at anything in particular,—just sends over each shot with a prayer, hoping that one of his strays will get some poor unsuspecting Fritz in the napper hundreds of yards behind the lines. It generally does; that's the reason the Boches hate the man from Erin's Isle.

The Saxons, though better than the Prussians and Bavarians, have a nasty trait of treachery in their make-up.

At one point of the line where the trenches were very close, a stake was driven into the ground midway between the hostile lines. At night when it was his turn, Tommy would crawl to this stake and attach some London papers to it, while at the foot he would place tins of bully beef, fags, sweets, and other delicacies that he had received from Blighty in the ever looked-for parcel. Later on Fritz would come out and get these luxuries.

The next night Tommy would go out to see what Fritz had put into his stocking. The donation generally consisted of a paper from Berlin, telling who was winning the war, some tinned sausages, cigars, and occasionally a little beer, but a funny thing, Tommy never returned with the beer unless it was inside of him. His platoon got a whiff of his breath one night and the offending Tommy lost his job.

One night a young English Sergeant crawled to the stake and as he tried to detach the German paper a bomb exploded and mangled him horribly. Fritz had set his trap and gained another victim which was only one more black mark against him in the book of this war. From that time on diplomatic relations were severed.

Returning to Tommy, I think his spirit is best shown in the questions he asks. It is never "who is going to win" but always "how long will it take?"

CHAPTER XX

"CHATS WITH FRITZ"

WE were swimming in money, from the receipts of our theatrical venture, and had forgotten all about the war, when an order came through that our Brigade would again take over their sector of the line.

The day that these orders were issued, our Captain assembled the company and asked for volunteers to go to the Machine Gun School at St. Omer. I volunteered and was accepted.

Sixteen men from our brigade left for the course in machine gunnery. This course lasted two weeks and we rejoined our unit and were assigned to the Brigade Machine Gun Company. It almost broke my heart to leave my company mates.

The gun we used was the Vickers, Light .303, water cooled.

I was still a member of the Suicide Club, having jumped from the frying pan into the fire. I was assigned to Section 1, Gun No. 2, and the first time "in" took position in the front-line trench.

During the day our gun would be dismounted on the fire step ready for instant use. We shared a dugout with the Lewis gunners, at "stand to" we would mount our gun on the parapet and go on watch beside it until "stand down" in the morning, then the gun would be dismounted and again placed in readiness on the fire step.

We did eight days in the front-line trench without anything unusual happening outside of the ordinary trench routine. On the night that we were to "carry out," a bombing raid against the German lines was pulled off. This raiding party consisted of sixty company men, sixteen bombers, and four Lewis machine guns with their crews.

The raid took the Boches by surprise and was a complete success, the party bringing back twenty-one prisoners.

The Germans must have been awfully sore, because they turned loose a barrage of shrapnel, with a few "Minnies" and "whizz bangs" intermixed. The shells were dropping into our front line like hailstones.

To get even, we could have left the prisoners in the fire trench, in charge of the men on guard and let them click Fritz's *strafeing* but Tommy does not treat prisoners that way.

Five of them were brought into my dugout and turned over to me so that they would be safe from the German fire.

In the candlelight, they looked very much shaken, nerves gone and chalky faces, with the exception of one, a great big fellow. He looked very much at ease. I liked him from the start.

I got out the rum jar and gave each a nip and passed around some fags, the old reliable Wood-bines. The other prisoners looked their gratitude, but the big fellow said in English, "Thank you, sir, the rum is excellent and I appreciate it, also your kindness."

He told me his name was Carl Schmidt, of the 66th Bavarian Light Infantry; that he had lived six years in New York (knew the city better than I did), had been to Coney Island and many of our ball games. He was a regular fan. I couldn't make him believe that Hans Wagner wasn't the best ball-player in the world.

From New York he had gone to London, where he worked as a waiter in the Hotel Russell. Just before the war he went home to Germany to see his parents, the war came and he was conscripted.

He told me he was very sorry to hear that London was in ruins from the Zeppelin raids. I could not convince him otherwise, for hadn't he seen moving pictures in one of the German cities of St. Paul's Cathedral in ruins.

I changed the subject because he was so stubborn in his belief. It was my intention to try and pump him for information as to the methods of the German snipers, who had been causing us trouble in the last few days.

I broached the subject and he shut up like a clam. After a few minutes he very innocently said:

"German snipers get paid rewards for killing the English."

I eagerly asked, "What are they?"

He answered:

"For killing or wounding an English private, the sniper gets one mark. For killing or wounding an English officer he gets five marks, but if he kills a Red Cap or English General, the sniper gets twenty-one days tied to the wheel of a limber as punishment for his carelessness."

Then he paused, waiting for me to bite, I suppose.

I bit all right and asked him why the sniper was

punished for killing an English general. With a smile he replied:

"Well, you see, if all the English generals were killed, there would be no one left to make costly mistakes."

I shut him up, he was getting too fresh for a prisoner. After a while he winked at me and I winked back, then the escort came to take the prisoners to the rear. I shook hands and wished him "The best of luck and a safe journey to Blighty."

I liked that prisoner, he was a fine fellow, had an Iron Cross, too. I advised him to keep it out of sight, or some Tommy would be sending it home to his girl in Blighty as a souvenir.

One dark and rainy night while on guard we were looking over the top from the fire step of our front-line trench, when we heard a noise immediately in front of our barbed wire. The sentry next to me challenged, "Halt, Who Comes There?" and brought his rifle to the aim. His challenge was answered in German. A captain in the next traverse climbed upon the sandbagged parapet to investigate—a brave but foolhardly deed—"Crack" went a bullet and he tumbled back into the trench with a hole through his stomach and died a few minutes later. A lance-corporal in the next platoon was so enraged at the Captain's death that he chucked a Mills bomb in the direction of the noise with the shouted warning to us; "Duck your nappers, my lucky lads." A sharp dynamite report, a flare in front of us, and then silence.

We immediately sent up two star shells, and in their light could see two dark forms lying on the ground close to our wire. A sergeant and four stretcher-bearers went out in front and soon returned, carrying two limp bodies. Down in the dugout, in the flickering light of three candles, we saw that they were two German officers, one a captain and the other an unteroffizier, a rank one grade higher than a sergeant-major, but below the grade of a lieutenant.

The Captain's face had been almost completely torn away by the bomb's explosion. The Unteroffizier was alive, breathing with difficulty. In a few minutes he opened his eyes and blinked in the glare of the candles.

The pair had evidently been drinking heavily, for the alcohol fumes were sickening and completely pervaded the dugout. I turned away in disgust, hating to see a man cross the Great Divide full of booze.

One of our officers could speak German and he questioned the dying man.

In a faint voice, interrupted by frequent hiccoughs, the Unteroffizier told his story.

There had been a drinking bout among the officers in one of the German dugouts, the main beverage being champagne. With a drunken leer he informed us that champagne was plentiful on their side and that it did not cost them anything either. About seven that night the conversation had turned to the "contemptible" English, and the Captain had made a wager that he would hang his cap on the English barbed wire to show his contempt for the English sentries. The wager was accepted. At eight o'clock the Captain and he had crept out into No Man's Land to carry out this wager.

They had gotten about half way across when the drink took effect and the Captain fell asleep. After about two hours of vain attempts the Unteroffizier had at last succeeded in waking the Captain, reminded him of his bet, and warned him that he would be the laughingstock of the officers' mess if he did not accomplish his object, but the

Captain was trembling all over and insisted on returning to the German lines. In the darkness they lost their bearings and crawled toward the English trenches. They reached the barbed wire and were suddenly challenged by our sentry. Being too drunk to realize that the challenge was in English, the Captain refused to crawl back. Finally the Unteroffizier convinced his superior that they were in front of the English wire. Realizing this too late, the Captain drew his revolver and with a muttered curse fired blindly toward our trench. His bullet no doubt killed our Captain.

Then the bomb came over and there he was, dying,—and a good job too, we thought. The Captain dead? Well, *his* men wouldn't weep at the news.

Without giving us any further information the Unteroffizier died.

We searched the bodies for identification disks but they had left everything behind before starting on their foolhardy errand.

Next afternoon we buried them in our little cemetery apart from the graves of the Tommies. If you ever go into that cemetery you will see two little wooden crosses in the corner of the cemetery set away from the rest.

They read:

> Captain
> German Army
> Died — 1916
> Unknown
> R. I. P.

> Unteroffizier
> German Army
> Died — 1916
> Unknown
> R. I. P.

CHAPTER XXI

ABOUT TURN

THE next evening we were relieved by the —th Brigade, and once again returned to rest billets. Upon arriving at these billets we were given twenty-four hours in which to clean up. I had just finished getting the mud from my uniform when the Orderly Sergeant informed me that my name was in orders for leave, and that I was to report to the Orderly Room in the morning for orders, transportation, and rations.

I nearly had a fit, hustled about, packing up, filling my pack with souvenirs such as shell heads, dud bombs, nose caps, shrapnel balls, and a Prussian Guardsman's helmet. In fact, before I turned in that night, I had everything ready to report at the Orderly Room at nine the next morning.

I was the envy of the whole section, swanking around, telling of the good time I was going to have, the places I would visit, and the real, old English beer I intended to guzzle. Sort of rubbed it into them, because they all do it, and now that it was my turn, I took pains to get my own back.

At nine I reported to the Captain, receiving my travel order and pass. He asked me how much money I wanted to draw. I glibly answered, "Three hundred francs, sir"; he just as glibly handed me one hundred.

Reporting at Brigade Headquarters, with my pack weighing a ton, I waited, with forty others, for the Adjutant to inspect us. After an hour's wait, he came out; must have been sore because he wasn't going with us.

The Quartermaster-Sergeant issued us two days' rations, in a little white canvas ration bag, which we tied to our belts.

Then two motor lorries came along and we piled in, laughing, joking, and in the best of spirits. We even loved the Germans, we were feeling so happy. Our journey to seven days' bliss in Blighty had commenced.

The ride in the lorry lasted about two hours; by this time we were covered with fine, white dust from the road, but didn't mind, even if we were nearly choking.

At the railroad station at F—— we reported to an officer, who had a white band around his arm, which read "R. T. O." (Royal Transportation Officer). To us this officer was Santa Claus.

The Sergeant in charge showed him our orders; he glanced through them and said, "Make yourselves comfortable on the platform and don't leave, the train is liable to be along in five minutes —or five hours."

It came in five hours, a string of eleven match boxes on big, high wheels, drawn by a dinky little engine with the "con." These match boxes were cattle cars, on the sides of which was painted the old familiar sign, "Hommes 40, Chevaux 8."

The R. T. O. stuck us all into one car. We didn't care, it was as good as a Pullman to us.

Two days we spent on that train, bumping, stopping, jerking ahead, and sometimes sliding back. At three stations we stopped long enough to make some tea, but were unable to wash, so when we arrived at B——, where we were to embark for Blighty, we were as black as Turcos and, with our unshaven faces, we looked like a lot of tramps. Though tired out, we were happy.

We had packed up, preparatory to detraining, when a R. T. O. held up his hand for us to stop where we were and came over. This is what he said:

"Boys, I'm sorry, but orders have just been received cancelling all leave. If you had been three hours earlier you would have gotten away. Just stay in that train, as it is going back. Rations will be issued to you for your return journey to your respective stations. Beastly rotten, I know." Then he left.

A dead silence resulted. Then men started to curse, threw their rifles on the floor of the car, others said nothing, seemed to be stupefied, while some had the tears running down their cheeks. It was a bitter disappointment to all.

How we blinded at the engineer of that train, it was all his fault (so we reasoned), why hadn't he speeded up a little or been on time, then we would have gotten off before the order arrived? Now it was no Blighty for us.

That return journey was misery to us; I just can't describe it.

When we got back to rest billets, we found that our Brigade was in the trenches (another agreeable surprise), and that an attack was contemplated.

Seventeen of the forty-one will never get

another chance to go on leave; they were killed in the attack. Just think if that train had been on time, those seventeen would still be alive.

I hate to tell you how I was kidded by the boys when I got back, but it was good and plenty.

Our Machine Gun Company took over their part of the line at seven o'clock, the night after I returned from my near leave.

At 3.30 the following morning three waves went over and captured the first and second German trenches. The machine gunners went over with the fourth wave to consolidate the captured line or "dig in" as Tommy calls it.

Crossing No Man's Land without clicking any casualties, we came to the German trench and mounted our guns on the parados of same.

I never saw such a mess in my life—bunches of twisted barbed wire lying about, shell holes everywhere, trench all bashed in, parapets gone, and dead bodies, why, that ditch was full of them, theirs and ours. It was a regular morgue. Some were mangled horribly from our shell fire, while others were wholly or partly buried in the mud, the result of shell explosions caving in the walls of the trench. One dead German was lying on his back, with a rifle sticking straight up in the air, the bayonet of which was buried to the hilt in his chest. Across his feet lay a dead English soldier with a bullet hole in his forehead. This Tommy must have been killed just as he ran his bayonet through the German.

Rifles and equipment were scattered about, and occasionally a steel helmet could be seen sticking out of the mud.

At one point, just in the entrance to a communication trench, was a stretcher. On this stretcher a German was lying with a white bandage around his knee, near to him lay one of the stretcher-bearers, the red cross on his arm covered with mud and his helmet filled with blood and brains. Close by, sitting up against the wall of the trench, with head resting on his chest, was the other stretcher-bearer. He seemed to be alive, the posture was so natural and easy, but when I got closer, I could see a large, jagged hole in his temple. The three must have been killed by the same shell-burst.

The dugouts were all smashed in and knocked about, big square-cut timbers splintered into bits, walls caved in, and entrances choked.

Tommy, after taking a trench, learns to his sorrow, that the hardest part of the work is to hold it.

In our case this proved to be so.

The German artillery and machine guns had us taped (ranged) for fair; it was worth your life to expose yourself an instant.

Don't think for a minute that the Germans were the only sufferers, we were clicking casualties so fast that you needed an adding machine to keep track of them.

Did you ever see one of the steam shovels at work on the Panama Canal, well, it would look like a hen scratching alongside of a Tommy "digging in" while under fire, you couldn't see daylight through the clouds of dirt from his shovel.

After losing three out of six men of our crew, we managed to set up our machine gun. One of the legs of the tripod was resting on the chest of a half-buried body. When the gun was firing, it gave the impression that the body was breathing, this was caused by the excessive vibration.

Three or four feet down the trench, about three feet from the ground, a foot was protruding from the earth; we knew it was a German by the black leather boot. One of our crew used that foot to hang extra bandoliers of ammunition on. This man always was a handy fellow; made use of little points that the ordinary person would over-look.

The Germans made three counter attacks, which we repulsed, but not without heavy loss on our side. They also suffered severely from our shell- and machine-gun fire. The ground was spotted with their dead and dying.

The next day things were somewhat quieter, but not quiet enough to bury the dead.

We lived, ate, and slept in that trench with the unburied dead for six days. It was awful to watch their faces become swollen and discolored. Towards the last the stench was fierce.

What got on my nerves the most was that foot sticking out of the dirt. It seemed to me, at night, in the moonlight, to be trying to twist around. Several times this impression was so strong that I went to it and grasped it in both hands, to see if I could feel a movement.

I told this to the man who had used it for a hat-rack just before I lay down for a little nap, as things were quiet and I needed a rest pretty badly. When I woke up the foot was gone. He had cut it off with our chain saw out of the spare parts' box, and had plastered the stump over with mud.

During the next two or three days, before we were relieved, I missed that foot dreadfully, seemed as if I had suddenly lost a chum.

I think the worst thing of all was to watch the rats, at night, and sometimes in the day, run over and play about among the dead.

Near our gun, right across the parapet, could be seen the body of a German lieutenant, the head and arms of which were hanging into our trench. The man who had cut off the foot used to sit and carry on a one-sided conversation with this officer, used to argue and point out why Germany was in the wrong. During all of this monologue, I never heard him say anything out of the way, anything that would have hurt the officer's feelings had he been alive. He was square all right, wouldn't even take advantage of a dead man in an argument.

To civilians this must seem dreadful, but out here, one gets so used to awful sights, that it makes no impression. In passing a butcher shop, you are not shocked by seeing a dead turkey hanging from a hook, well, in France, a dead body is looked upon from the same angle.

But, nevertheless, when our six days were up, we were tickled to death to be relieved.

Our Machine Gun Company lost seventeen

killed and thirty-one wounded in that little local affair of "straightening the line," while the other companies clicked it worse than we did.

After the attack we went into reserve billets for six days, and on the seventh once again we were in rest billets.

CHAPTER XXII

PUNISHMENTS AND MACHINE-GUN STUNTS

SOON after my arrival in France, in fact from my enlistment, I had found that in the British Army discipline is very strict. One has to be very careful in order to stay on the narrow path of government virtue.

There are about seven million ways of breaking the King's Regulations; to keep one you have to break another.

The worst punishment is death by a firing squad or "up against the wall" as Tommy calls it.

This is for desertion, cowardice, mutiny, giving information to the enemy, destroying or willfully wasting ammunition, looting, rape, robbing the dead, forcing a safeguard, striking a superior, etc.

Then comes the punishment of sixty-four days in the front-line trench without relief. During this time you have to engage in all raids, working parties in No Man's Land, and every hazardous undertaking that comes along. If you live through the sixty-four days you are indeed lucky.

This punishment is awarded where there is a doubt as to the willful guilt of a man who has committed an offence punishable by death.

Then comes the famous Field Punishment No. 1. Tommy has nicknamed it "crucifixion." It means that a man is spread eagled on a limber wheel, two hours a day for twenty-one days. During this time he only gets water, bully beef, and biscuits for his chow. You get "crucified" for repeated minor offences.

Next in order is Field Punishment No. 2.

This is confinement in the "Clink," without blankets, getting water, bully beef, and biscuits for rations and doing all the dirty work that can be found. This may be for twenty-four hours or twenty days, according to the gravity of the offence.

Then comes "Pack Drill" or Defaulters' Parade. This consists of drilling, mostly at the double, for two hours with full equipment. Tommy hates this, because it is hard work. Sometimes he fills his pack with straw to lighten it, and sometimes he gets caught. If he gets caught, he grouses at everything in general for twenty-one days, from the vantage point of a limber wheel.

Next comes "C. B." meaning "Confined to

Barracks." This consists of staying in billets or barracks for twenty-four hours to seven days. You also get an occasional Defaulters' Parade and dirty jobs around the quarters.

The Sergeant-Major keeps what is known as the Crime Sheet. When a man commits an offence, he is "Crimed," that is, his name, number, and offence is entered on the Crime Sheet. Next day at 9 A.M. he goes to the "Orderly Room" before the Captain, who either punishes him with "C. B." or sends him before the O. C. (Officer Commanding Battalion). The Captain of the Company can only award "C. B."

Tommy many a time has thanked the King for making that provision in his regulations.

To gain the title of a "smart soldier," Tommy has to keep clear of the Crime Sheet, and you have to be darned smart to do it.

I have been on it a few times, mostly for "Yankee impudence."

During our stay of two weeks in rest billets our Captain put us through a course of machine-gun drills, trying out new stunts and theories.

After parades were over, our guns' crews got together and also tried out some theories of their own in reference to handling guns. These courses had nothing to do with the advancement of the war, consisted mostly of causing tricky jams in the gun, and then the rest of the crew would endeavor to locate as quickly as possible the cause of the stoppage. This amused them for a few days and then things came to a standstill.

One of the boys on my gun claimed that he could play a tune while the gun was actually firing, and demonstrated this fact one day on the target range. We were very enthusiastic and decided to become musicians.

After constant practice I became quite expert in the tune entitled *All Conductors Have Big Feet.*

When I had mastered this tune, our two weeks' rest came to an end, and once again we went up the line and took over the sector in front of G—— Wood.

At this point the German trenches ran around the base of a hill, on the top of which was a dense wood. This wood was infested with machine guns, which used to traverse our lines at will, and sweep the streets of a little village, where we were billeted while in reserve.

There was one gun in particular which used to get our goats, it had the exact range of our "ele-

phant" dugout entrance, and every evening, about
the time rations were being brought up, its bullets
would knock up the dust on the road; more than
one Tommy went West or to Blighty by running
into them.

This gun got our nerves on edge, and Fritz
seemed to know it, because he never gave us an
hour's rest. Our reputation as machine gunners
was at stake; we tried various ruses to locate and
put this gun out of action, but each one proved to
be a failure, and Fritz became a worse nuisance
than ever. He was getting fresher and more
careless every day, took all kinds of liberties,
with us,—thought he was invincible.

Then one of our crew got a brilliant idea and we
were all enthusiastic to put it to the test.

Here was his scheme:

When firing my gun, I was to play my tune, and
Fritz, no doubt, would fall for it, try to imitate
me as an added insult. This gunner and two
others would try, by the sound, to locate Fritz
and his gun. After having got the location, they
would mount two machine guns in trees, in a little
clump of woods, to the left of our cemetery, and
while Fritz was in the middle of his lesson, would
open up and trust to luck. By our calculations,

it would take at least a week to pull off the stunt.

If Fritz refused to swallow our bait, it would be impossible to locate his special gun, and that's the one we were after, because they all sound alike, a slow pup-pup-pup.

Our prestige was hanging by a thread. In the battalion we had to endure all kinds of insults and fresh remarks as to our ability in silencing Fritz. Even to the battalion that German gun was a sore spot.

Next day, Fritz opened up as usual. I let him fire away for a while and then butted in with my "pup-pup-pup-pup-pup-pup." I kept this up quite a while, used two belts of ammunition. Fritz had stopped firing to listen. Then he started in; sure enough, he had fallen for our game, his gun was trying to imitate mine, but, at first he made a horrible mess of that tune. Again I butted in with a few bars and stopped. Then he tried to copy what I had played. He was a good sport all right, because his bullets were going away over our heads, must have been firing into the air. I commenced to feel friendly toward him.

This duet went on for five days. Fritz was a good pupil and learned rapidly, in fact, got better than his teacher. I commenced to feel jealous. When he had completely mastered the tune, he started sweeping the road again and we clicked it worse than ever. But he signed his death warrant by doing so, because my friendship turned to hate. Every time he fired he played that tune and we danced.

The boys in the battalion gave us the "Ha! Ha!" They weren't in on our little frame-up.

The originator of the ruse and the other two gunners had Fritz's location taped to the minute; they mounted their two guns, and also gave me the range. The next afternoon was set for the grand finale.

Our three guns, with different elevations, had their fire so arranged, that, opening up together, their bullets would suddenly drop on Fritz like a hailstorm.

About three the next day, Fritz started "pup-pupping" that tune. I blew a sharp blast on a whistle, it was the signal agreed upon; we turned loose and Fritz's gun suddenly stopped in the middle of a bar. We had cooked his goose, and our ruse had worked. After firing two belts each, to make sure of our job, we hurriedly dismounted our guns and took cover in the dugout. We knew what to expect soon. We didn't have to wait long, three salvos of "whizz-bangs" came over from Fritz's artillery, a further confirmation that we had sent that musical machine-gunner on his westward bound journey.

That gun never bothered us again. We were the heroes of the battalion, our Captain congratulated us, said it was a neat piece of work, and, consequently, we were all puffed up over the stunt.

There are several ways Tommy uses to disguise the location of his machine gun and get his range. Some of the most commonly used stunts are as follows:

At night, when he mounts his gun over the top of his trench and wants to get the range of Fritz's trench he adopts the method of what he terms "getting the sparks." This consists of firing bursts from his gun until the bullets hit the German barbed wire. He can tell when they are cutting the wire, because a bullet when it hits a wire throws out a blue electric spark. Machine-gun fire is very damaging to wire and causes many a wiring party to go out at night when it is quiet to repair the damage.

To disguise the flare of his gun at night when firing, Tommy uses what is called a flare protector.

This is a stove-pipe arrangement which fits over the barrel casing of the gun and screens the sparks from the right and left, but not from the front. So Tommy, always resourceful, adopts this scheme. About three feet or less in front of the gun he drives two stakes into the ground, about five feet apart. Across these stakes he stretches a curtain made out of empty sandbags ripped open. He soaks this curtain in water and fires through it. The water prevents it catching fire and effectively screens the flare of the firing gun from the enemy.

Sound is a valuable asset in locating a machine gun, but Tommy surmounts this obstacle by placing two machine guns about one hundred to one hundred fifty yards apart. The gun on the right to cover with its fire the sector of the left gun and the gun on the left to cover that of the right gun. This makes their fire cross; they are fired simultaneously.

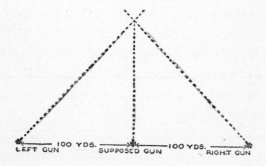

LEFT GUN ——— 100 YDS. ——— SUPPOSED GUN ——— 100 YDS. ——— RIGHT GUN

By this method it sounds like one gun firing and gives the Germans the impression that the gun is firing from a point midway between the guns which are actually firing, and they accordingly shell that particular spot. The machine gunners chuckle and say, "Fritz is a brainy boy, not 'alf he ain't."

But the men in our lines at the spot being shelled curse Fritz for his ignorance and pass a few pert remarks down the line in reference to the machine gunners being "windy" and afraid to take their medicine.

CHAPTER XXIII

GAS ATTACKS AND SPIES

THREE days after we had silenced Fritz, the Germans sent over gas. It did not catch us unawares, because the wind had been made to order, that is, it was blowing from the German trenches towards ours at the rate of about five miles per hour.

Warnings had been passed down the trench to keep a sharp lookout for gas.

We had a new man at the periscope, on this afternoon in question; I was sitting on the fire step, cleaning my rifle, when he called out to me:

"There's a sort of greenish, yellow cloud rolling along the ground out in front, it's coming——"

But I waited for no more, grabbing my bayonet, which was detached from the rifle, I gave the alarm by banging an empty shell case, which was hanging near the periscope. At the same instant, gongs started ringing down the trench, the signal

for Tommy to don his respirator, or smoke helmet,
as we call it.

Gas travels quickly, so you must not lose any
time; you generally have about eighteen or twenty
seconds in which to adjust your gas helmet.

A gas helmet is made of cloth, treated with
chemicals. There are two windows, or glass eyes,
in it, through which you can see. Inside there is
a rubber-covered tube, which goes in the mouth.
You breathe through your nose; the gas, passing
through the cloth helmet, is neutralized by the
action of the chemicals. The foul air is exhaled
through the tube in the mouth, this tube being
so constructed that it prevents the inhaling of
the outside air or gas. One helmet is good for
five hours of the strongest gas. Each Tommy
carries two of them slung around his shoulder
in a waterproof canvas bag. He must wear this
bag at all times, even while sleeping. To change
a defective helmet, you take out the new one,
hold your breath, pull the old one off, placing the
new one over your head, tucking in the loose ends
under the collar of your tunic.

For a minute, pandemonium reigned in our
trench,—Tommies adjusting their helmets, bombers running here and there, and men turning out

of the dugouts with fixed bayonets, to man the fire step.

Re-inforcements were pouring out of the communication trenches.

Our gun's crew were busy mounting the machine gun on the parapet and bringing up extra ammunition from the dugout.

German gas is heavier than air and soon fills the trenches and dugouts, where it has been known to lurk for two or three days, until the air is purified by means of large chemical sprayers.

We had to work quickly, as Fritz generally follows the gas with an infantry attack.

A company man on our right was too slow in getting on his helmet; he sank to the ground, clutching at his throat, and after a few spasmodic twistings, went West (died). It was horrible to see him die, but we were powerless to help him. In the corner of a traverse, a little, muddy cur dog, one of the company's pets, was lying dead, with his two paws over his nose.

It's the animals that suffer the most, the horses, mules, cattle, dogs, cats, and rats, they having no helmets to save them. Tommy does not sympathize with rats in a gas attack.

At times, gas has been known to travel, with dire results, fifteen miles behind the lines.

A gas, or smoke helmet, as it is called, at the best is a vile-smelling thing, and it is not long before one gets a violent headache from wearing it.

Our eighteen-pounders were bursting in No Man's Land, in an effort, by the artillery, to disperse the gas clouds.

The fire step was lined with crouching men, bayonets fixed, and bombs near at hand to repel the expected attack.

Our artillery had put a barrage of curtain fire on the German lines, to try and break up their attack and keep back re-inforcements.

I trained my machine gun on their trench and its bullets were raking the parapet.

Then over they came, bayonets glistening. In their respirators, which have a large snout in front, they looked like some horrible nightmare.

All along our trench, rifles and machine guns spoke, our shrapnel was bursting over their heads. They went down in heaps, but new ones took the place of the fallen. Nothing could stop that mad rush. The Germans reached our barbed wire, which had previously been demolished by their

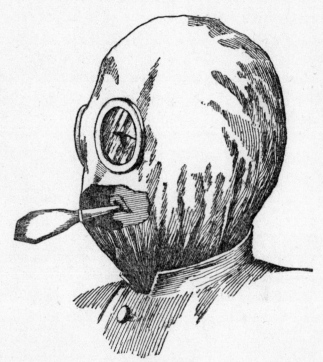

A Gas Helmet.

shells, then it was bomb against bomb, and the devil for all.

Suddenly, my head seemed to burst from a loud "crack" in my ear. Then my head began to swim, throat got dry, and a heavy pressure on the lungs warned me that my helmet was leaking. Turning my gun over to No. 2, I changed helmets.

The trench started to wind like a snake, and sandbags appeared to be floating in the air. The noise was horrible; I sank onto the fire step, needles seemed to be pricking my flesh, then blackness.

I was awakened by one of my mates removing my smoke helmet. How delicious that cool, fresh air felt in my lungs.

A strong wind had arisen and dispersed the gas.

They told me that I had been "out" for three hours; they thought I was dead.

The attack had been repulsed after a hard fight. Twice the Germans had gained a foothold in our trench, but had been driven out by counter-attacks. The trench was filled with their dead and ours. Through a periscope, I counted eighteen dead Germans in our wire; they were a ghastly sight in their horrible-looking respirators.

I examined my first smoke helmet, a bullet had gone through it on the left side, just grazing my ear, the gas had penetrated through the hole made in the cloth.

Out of our crew of six, we lost two killed and two wounded.

That night we buried all of the dead, excepting those in No Man's Land. In death there is not much distinction, friend and foe are treated alike.

After the wind had dispersed the gas, the R. A. M. C. got busy with their chemical sprayers, spraying out the dugouts and low parts of the trenches to dissipate any fumes of the German gas which may have been lurking in same.

Two days after the gas attack, I was sent to Division Headquarters, in answer to an order requesting that captains of units should detail a man whom they thought capable of passing an examination for the Divisional Intelligence Department.

Before leaving for this assignment I went along the front-line trench saying good-bye to my mates and lording it over them, telling them that I had clicked a cushy job behind the lines, and how sorry I felt that they had to stay in the front line and argue out the war with Fritz. They were envious but still good natured, and as I left the trench to go to the rear they shouted after me:

"Good luck, Yank, old boy, don't forget to send up a few fags to your old mates."

I promised to do this and left.

I reported at Headquarters with sixteen others and passed the required examination. Out of the sixteen applicants four were selected.

I was highly elated because I was, as I thought, in for a cushy job back at the base.

The next morning the four reported to Division Headquarters for instructions. Two of the men were sent to large towns in the rear of the lines with an easy job. When it came our turn, the officer told us we were good men and had passed a very creditable examination.

My tin hat began to get too small for me, and I noted that the other man, Atwell, by name, was sticking his chest out more than usual.

The officer continued: "I think I can use you two men to great advantage in the front line. Here are your orders and instructions, also the pass which gives you full authority as special M. P. detailed on intelligence work. Report at the front line according to your instructions. It is risky work and I wish you both the best of luck."

My heart dropped to zero and Atwell's face was a study. We saluted and left.

That wishing us the "best of luck" sounded very ominous in our ears; if he had said "I wish you both a swift and painless death" it would have been more to the point.

When we had read our instructions we knew we were in for it good and plenty.

What Atwell said is not fit for publication, but I strongly seconded his opinion of the War, Army, and Divisional Headquarters in general.

After a bit our spirits rose. We were full-fledged spy-catchers, because our instructions and orders said so.

We immediately reported to the nearest French *estaminet* and had several glasses of muddy water, which they called beer. After drinking our beer we left the *estaminet* and hailed an empty ambulance.

After showing the driver our passes we got in. The driver was going to the part of the line where we had to report.

The ambulance was a Ford and lived up to its reputation.

How the wounded ever survived a ride in it was inexplicable to me. It was worse than riding on a gun carriage over a rocky road.

The driver of the ambulance was a corporal of the R. A. M. C., and he had the "wind up," that is, he had an aversion to being under fire.

I was riding on the seat with him while Atwell was sitting in the ambulance, with his legs hanging out of the back.

As we passed through a shell-destroyed village a mounted military policeman stopped us and informed the driver to be very careful when we got out on the open road, as it was very dangerous, because the Germans lately had acquired the habit of shelling it. The Corporal asked the trooper if there was any other way around, and was informed that there was not. Upon this he got very nervous, and wanted to turn back, but we insisted that he proceed and explained to him that he would get into serious trouble with his commanding officer if he returned without orders; we wanted to ride, not walk.

From his conversation we learned that he had recently come from England with a draft and had never been under fire, hence, his nervousness.

We convinced him that there was not much danger, and he appeared greatly relieved.

When we at last turned into the open road, we were not so confident. On each side there

had been a line of trees, but now, all that was
left of them were torn and battered stumps.
The fields on each side of the road were dotted
with recent shell holes, and we passed several in
the road itself. We had gone about half a mile
when a shell came whistling through the air,
and burst in a field about three hundred yards to
our right. Another soon followed this one, and
burst on the edge of the road about four hundred
yards in front of us.

I told the driver to throw in his speed clutch, as
we must be in sight of the Germans. I knew the
signs: that battery was ranging for us, and the
quicker we got out of its zone of fire the better.
The driver was trembling like a leaf, and every
minute I expected him to pile us up in the ditch.
I preferred the German fire.

In the back, Atwell was holding onto the straps
for dear life, and was singing at the top of his
voice,

> We beat you at the Marne,
>   We beat you at the Aisne,
> We gave you hell at Neuve Chapelle,
>   And here we are again.

Just then we hit a small shell hole and nearly

capsized.   Upon a loud yell from the rear I looked behind, and there was Atwell sitting in the middle of the road, shaking his fist at us.   His equipment, which he had taken off upon getting into the ambulance, was strung out on the ground, and his rifle was in the ditch.

I shouted to the driver to stop, and in his nervousness he put on the brakes.   We nearly pitched out head first.   But the applying of those brakes saved our lives.   The next instant there was a blinding flash and a deafening report.   All that I remember is that I was flying through the air, and wondering if I would land in a soft spot.   Then the lights went out.

When I came to, Atwell was pouring water on my head out of his bottle.   On the other side of the road, the Corporal was sitting, rubbing a lump on his forehead with his left hand, while his right arm was bound up in a blood-soaked bandage. He was moaning very loudly.   I had an awful headache, and the skin on the left side of my face was full of gravel, and the blood was trickling from my nose.

But that ambulance was turned over in the ditch, and was perforated with holes from fragments of the shell.   One of the front wheels was slowly revolving, so I could not have been "out" for a long period.

If Mr. Ford could have seen that car, his "Peace at Any Price" conviction would have been materially strengthened, and he would have immediately fitted out another "peace ship."

The shells were still screaming overhead, but the battery had raised its fire, and they were bursting in a little wood, about half a mile from us.

Atwell spoke up, "I wish that officer hadn't wished us the best o' luck." Then he commenced swearing. I couldn't help laughing, though my head was nigh to bursting.

Slowly rising to my feet I felt myself all over to make sure that there were no broken bones. But outside of a few bruises and scratches, I was all right. The Corporal was still moaning, but more from shock than pain. A shell splinter had gone through the flesh of his right forearm. At-well and I, from our first-aid pouches, put a tourniquet on his arm to stop the bleeding, and then gathered up our equipment.

We realized that we were in a dangerous spot. At any minute a shell might drop on the road and finish us off. The village we had left was not very far, so we told the Corporal he had better go back to it and get his arm dressed, and then report the fact of the destruction of the ambulance to the military police. He was well able to walk, so he set off in the direction of the village, while Atwell and I continued our way on foot.

Without further mishap we arrived at our destination, and reported to Brigade Headquarters for rations and billets.

That night we slept in the Battalion Sergeant-Major's dugout. The next morning I went to a first-aid post and had the gravel picked out of my face.

The instructions we received from Division Headquarters read that we were out to catch spies, patrol trenches, search German dead, reconnoiter in No Man's Land, and take part in trench raids, and prevent the robbing of the dead.

I had a pass which would allow me to go anywhere at any time in the sector of the line held by our division. It also gave me authority to stop and search ambulances, motor lorries, wagons, and even officers and soldiers, whenever my suspicions deemed it necessary. Atwell and I were allowed to work together or singly,—it was left to our judgment. We decided to team up.

Atwell was a good companion and very entertaining. He had an utter contempt for danger, but was not foolhardy. At swearing he was a wonder. A cavalry regiment would have been proud of him. Though born in England, he had spent several years in New York. He was about six feet one, and as strong as an ox. I am five feet five in height, so we looked like "Bud" Fisher's "Mutt and Jeff" when together.

We took up our quarters in a large dugout of the Royal Engineers, and mapped out our future actions. This dugout was on the edge of a large cemetery, and several times at night in returning to it, we got many a fall stumbling over the graves of English, French, and Germans. Atwell on these occasions never indulged in swearing, though at any other time, at the least stumble, he would turn the air blue.

A certain section of our trenches was held by the Royal Irish Rifles. For several days a very strong rumor went the rounds that a German spy was in our midst. This spy was supposed to be dressed in the uniform of a British Staff Officer. Several stories had been told about an officer wearing a red band around his cap, who patrolled the front-line and communication trenches asking suspicious questions as to location of batteries, machine-gun emplacements, and trench mortars. If a shell dropped in a battery, on a machine gun, or even near a dugout, this spy was blamed.

The rumor gained such strength that an order was issued for all troops to immediately place under arrest anyone answering to the description of the spy.

Atwell and I were on the *qui vive*. We constantly patrolled the trenches at night, and even in the day, but the spy always eluded us.

One day, while in a communication trench, we were horrified to see our Brigadier-General, Old Pepper, being brought down it by a big private of the Royal Irish Rifles. The General was walking in front, and the private with fixed bayonet was following him in the rear.

We saluted as the General passed us. The Irishman had a broad grin on his face and we could scarcely believe our eyes—the General was under arrest. After passing a few feet beyond us, the General turned, and said in a wrathful voice to Atwell:

"Tell this d—n fool who I am. He's arrested me as a spy."

Atwell was speechless. The sentry butted in with:

"None o' that gassin' out o' you. Back to Headquarters you goes, Mr. Fritz. Open that face o' yours again, an' I'll dent in your napper with the butt o' me rifle."

The General's face was a sight to behold. He was fairly boiling over with rage, but he shut up.

Atwell tried to get in front of the sentry to explain to him that it really was the General he had under arrest, but the sentry threatened to run his bayonet through him, and would have done it, too. So Atwell stepped aside, and remained silent. I was nearly bursting with suppressed laughter. One word, and I would have exploded. It is not exactly diplomatic to laugh at your General in such a predicament.

The sentry and his prisoner arrived at Brigade Headquarters with disastrous results to the sentry.

The joke was that the General had personally issued the order for the spy's arrest. It was a habit of the General to walk through the trenches on rounds of inspection, unattended by any of his staff. The Irishman, being new in the regiment, had never seen the General before, so when he came across him alone in a communication trench, he promptly put him under arrest. Brigadier-generals wear a red band around their caps.

Next day we passed the Irishman tied to the wheel of a limber, the beginning of his sentence of twenty-one days, Field Punishment No. 1. Never before have I seen such a woebegone expression on a man's face.

For several days, Atwell and I made ourselves scarce around Brigade Headquarters. We did not want to meet the General.

The spy was never caught.

CHAPTER XXIV

THE FIRING SQUAD

A FEW days later I had orders to report back to Divisional Headquarters, about thirty kilos behind the line. I reported to the A. P. M. (Assistant Provost Marshal). He told me to report to billet No. 78 for quarters and rations.

It was about eight o'clock at night and I was tired and soon fell asleep in the straw of the billet. It was a miserable night outside, cold, and a drizzly rain was falling.

About two in the morning I was awakened by someone shaking me by the shoulder. Opening my eyes I saw a Regimental Sergeant-Major bending over me. He had a lighted lantern in his right hand. I started to ask him what was the matter, when he put his finger to his lips for silence and whispered:

"Get on your equipment, and, without any noise, come with me."

This greatly mystified me, but I obeyed his order.

Outside of the billet, I asked him what was up, but he shut me up with:

"Don't ask any questions, it's against orders. I don't know myself."

It was raining like the mischief.

We splashed along a muddy road for about fifteen minutes, finally stopping at the entrance of what must have been an old barn. In the darkness, I could hear pigs grunting, as if they had just been disturbed. In front of the door stood an officer in a mack (mackintosh). The R. S. M. went up to him, whispered something, and then left. This officer called to me, asked my name, number and regiment, at the same time, in the light of a lantern he was holding, making a notation in a little book.

When he had finished writing, he whispered:

"Go into that billet and wait orders, and no talking. Understand?"

I stumbled into the barn and sat on the floor in the darkness. I could see no one, but could hear men breathing and moving; they seemed nervous and restless. I know I was.

During my wait, three other men entered.

Then the officer poked his head in the door and ordered:

"Fall in, outside the billet, in single rank."

We fell in, standing at ease. Then he commanded.

"Squad—'Shun! Number!"

There were twelve of us.

"Right — Turn! Left — Wheel! Quick — March!" And away we went. The rain was trickling down my back and I was shivering from the cold.

With the officer leading, we must have marched over an hour, plowing through the mud and occasionally stumbling into a shell hole in the road, when suddenly the officer made a left wheel, and we found ourselves in a sort of enclosed courtyard.

The dawn was breaking and the rain had ceased.

In front of us were four stacks of rifles, three to a stack.

The officer brought us to attention and gave the order to unpile arms. We each took a rifle. Giving us "Stand at ease," in a nervous and shaky voice, he informed:

"Men, you are here on a very solemn duty.

You have been selected as a firing squad for the execution of a soldier, who, having been found guilty of a grievous crime against King and Country, has been regularly and duly tried and sentenced to be shot at 3.28 A.M. this date. This sentence has been approved by the reviewing authority and ordered carried out. It is our duty to carry on with the sentence of the court.

"There are twelve rifles, one of which contains a blank cartridge, the other eleven containing ball cartridges. Every man is expected to do his duty and fire to kill. Take your orders from me. Squad—'Shun!'"

We came to attention. Then he left. My heart was of lead and my knees shook.

After standing at "Attention" for what seemed a week, though in reality it could not have been over five minutes, we heard a low whispering in our rear and footsteps on the stone flagging of the courtyard.

Our officer reappeared and in a low, but firm voice, ordered:

"About—Turn!"

We turned about. In the gray light of dawn, a few yards in front of me, I could make out a brick wall. Against this wall was a dark form with a white square pinned on its breast. We were supposed to aim at this square. To the right of the form I noticed a white spot on the wall. This would be my target.

"Ready! Aim! Fire!"

The dark form sank into a huddled heap. My bullet sped on its way, and hit the whitish spot on the wall; I could see the splinters fly. Someone else had received the rifle containing the blank cartridge, but my mind was at ease, there was no blood of a Tommy on my hands.

"Order—Arms! About—Turn! Pile—Arms! Stand—Clear."

The stacks were re-formed.

"Quick—March! Right—Wheel!" and we left the scene of execution behind us.

It was now daylight. After marching about five minutes, we were dismissed with the following instructions from the officer in command:

"Return, alone, to your respective companies, and remember, no talking about this affair, or else it will go hard with the guilty ones."

We needed no urging to get away. I did not recognize any of the men on the firing squad, even the officer was a stranger to me.

The victim's relations and friends in Blighty will

never know that he was executed; they will be under the impression that he died doing his bit for King and Country.

In the public casualty lists his name will appear under the caption "Accidentally Killed," or "Died."

The day after the execution I received orders to report back to the line, and to keep a still tongue in my head.

Executions are a part of the day's work but the part we hated most of all, I think—certainly the saddest. The British War Department is thought by many people to be composed of rigid regulations all wound around with red tape. But it has a heart, and one of the evidences of this is the considerate way in which an execution is concealed and reported to the relative of the unfortunate man. They never know the truth. He is listed in the bulletins as among the "accidentally killed."

In the last ten years I have several times read stories in magazines of cowards changing, in a charge, to heroes. I used to laugh at it. It seemed easy for story-writers but I said, "Men aren't made that way." But over in France I learned once that the streak of yellow can turn all white. I picked up the story, bit by bit, from the Captain of the Company, the sentries who guarded the poor fellow, as well as from my own observations. At first I did not realize the whole of his story, but after a week of investigation it stood out as clear in my mind as the mountains of my native West in the spring sunshine. It impressed me so much that I wrote it all down in rest billets on odd scraps of paper. The incidents are, as I say, every bit true; the feelings of the man are true,—I know from all I underwent in the fighting over in France.

We will call him Albert Lloyd. That wasn't his name, but it will do:

Albert Lloyd was what the world terms a coward.

In London they called him a slacker

His country had been at war nearly eighteen months, and still he was not in khaki.

He had no good reason for not enlisting, being alone in the world, having been educated in an Orphan Asylum, and there being no one dependent upon him for support. He had no good position to lose, and there was no sweetheart to tell him with her lips to go, while her eyes pleaded for him to stay.

Every time he saw a recruiting sergeant, he'd slink around the corner out of sight, with a terrible fear gnawing at his heart. When passing the big recruiting posters, and on his way to business and back he passed many, he would pull down his cap and look the other way, to get away from that awful finger pointing at him, under the caption, "Your King and Country Need You"; or the boring eyes of Kitchener, which burned into his very soul, causing him to shudder.

Then the Zeppelin raids—during them, he used to crouch in a corner of his boarding-house cellar, whimpering like a whipped puppy and calling upon the Lord to protect him.

Even his landlady despised him, although she had to admit that he was "good pay."

He very seldom read the papers, but one momentous morning, the landlady put the morning paper at his place before he came down to breakfast. Taking his seat, he read the flaring headline, "Conscription Bill Passed," and nearly fainted. Excusing himself, he stumbled upstairs to his bedroom, with the horror of it gnawing into his vitals.

Having saved up a few pounds, he decided not to leave the house, and to sham sickness, so he stayed in his room and had the landlady serve his meals there.

Everytime there was a knock at the door, he trembled all over, imagining it was a policeman who had come to take him away to the army.

One morning his fears were realized. Sure enough there stood a policeman with the fatal paper. Taking it in his trembling hand, he read that he, Albert Lloyd, was ordered to report himself to the nearest recruiting station for physical examination. He reported immediately, because he was afraid to disobey.

The doctor looked with approval upon Lloyd's six feet of physical perfection, and thought what a fine guardsman he would make, but examined his heart twice before he passed him as "physically fit"; it was beating so fast.

From the recruiting depot Lloyd was taken, with many others, in charge of a sergeant, to the training depot at Aldershot, where he was given an outfit of khaki, and drew his other equipment. He made a fine-looking soldier, except for the slight shrinking in his shoulders, and the hunted look in his eyes.

At the training depot it does not take long to find out a man's character, and Lloyd was promptly dubbed "Windy." In the English Army, "windy" means cowardly.

The smallest recruit in the barracks looked on him with contempt, and was not slow to show it in many ways.

Lloyd was a good soldier, learned quickly, obeyed every order promptly, never groused at the hardest fatigues. He was afraid to. He lived in deadly fear of the officers and "Non-Coms" over him. They also despised him.

One morning about three months after his enlistment, Lloyd's company was paraded, and the names picked for the next draft to France were read. When his name was called, he did not step out smartly, two paces to the front, and answer cheerfully, "Here, sir," as the others did. He just fainted in ranks, and was carried to barracks amid the sneers of the rest.

That night was an agony of misery to him. He could not sleep. Just cried and whimpered in his bunk, because on the morrow the draft was to sail for France, where he would see death on all sides, and perhaps be killed himself. On the steamer, crossing the Channel, he would have jumped overboard to escape, but was afraid of drowning.

Arriving in France, he and the rest were huddled into cattle cars. On the side of each appeared in white letters, "Chevaux 8, Hommes 40." After hours of bumping over the uneven French road beds they arrived at the training base of Rouen.

At this place they were put through a week's rigid training in trench warfare. On the morning of the eighth day, they paraded at ten o'clock, and were inspected and passed by General H——, then were marched to the Quartermaster's, to draw their gas helmets and trench equipment.

At four in the afternoon, they were again hustled into cattle cars. This time, the journey lasted two days. They disembarked at the town of Frévent, and could hear a distant dull booming. With knees shaking, Lloyd asked the Sergeant what the noise was, and nearly dropped when the Sergeant replied in a somewhat bored tone:

"Oh, them's the guns up the line. We'll be up there in a couple o' days or so. Don't worry, my laddie, you'll see more of 'em than you want before you get 'ome to Blighty again, that is, if you're lucky enough to get back. Now lend a hand there unloadin' them cars, and quit that everlastin' shakin'. I believe yer scared." The last with a contemptuous sneer.

They marched ten kilos, full pack, to a little dilapidated village, and the sound of the guns grew louder, constantly louder.

The village was full of soldiers who turned out to inspect the new draft, the men who were shortly to be their mates in the trenches, for they were going "up the line" on the morrow, to "take over" their certain sector of trenches.

The draft was paraded in front of Battalion Headquarters, and the men were assigned to companies.

Lloyd was the only man assigned to "D" Company. Perhaps the officer in charge of the draft had something to do with it, for he called Lloyd aside, and said:

"Lloyd, you are going to a new company. No one knows you. Your bed will be as you make it, so for God's sake, brace up and be a man. I think you have the stuff in you, my boy, so good-bye, and the best of luck to you."

The next day the battalion took over their part of the trenches. It happened to be a very quiet day. The artillery behind the lines was still, except for an occasional shell sent over to let the Germans know the gunners were not asleep.

In the darkness, in single file, the Company slowly wended their way down the communication trench to the front line. No one noticed Lloyd's white and drawn face.

After they had relieved the Company in the trenches, Lloyd, with two of the old company men, was put on guard in one of the traverses. Not a shot was fired from the German lines, and no one paid any attention to him crouched on the firing step.

On the first time in, a new recruit is not required to stand with his head "over the top." He only "sits it out," while the older men keep watch.

At about ten o'clock, all of a sudden, he thought hell had broken loose, and crouched and shivered up against the parapet. Shells started bursting, as he imagined, right in their trench, when in fact they were landing about a hundred yards in rear of them, in the second lines.

One of the older men on guard, turning to his mate, said:

"There goes Fritz with those damned trench mortars again. It's about time our artillery 'taped' them, and sent over a few. Well, I'll be damned, where's that blighter of a draft man gone to? There's his rifle leaning against the

parapet. He must have legged it. Just keep
your eye peeled, Dick, while I report it to the
Sergeant. I wonder if the fool knows he can be
shot for such tricks as leavin' his post."

Lloyd had gone. When the trench mortars
opened up, a maddening terror seized him and he
wanted to run, to get away from that horrible
din, anywhere to safety. So quietly sneaking
around the traverse, he came to the entrance of a
communication trench, and ran madly and blindly
down it, running into traverses, stumbling into
muddy holes, and falling full length over trench
grids.

Groping blindly, with his arms stretched out in
front of him, he at last came out of the trench into
the village, or what used to be a village, before
the German artillery razed it.

Mixed with his fear, he had a peculiar sort of
cunning, which whispered to him to avoid all
sentries, because if they saw him he would be
sent back to that awful destruction in the front
line, and perhaps be killed or maimed. The
thought made him shudder, the cold sweat coming
out in beads on his face.

On his left, in the darkness, he could make
out the shadowy forms of trees; crawling on his

hands and knees, stopping and crouching with fear at each shell-burst, he finally reached an old orchard, and cowered at the base of a shot-scarred apple-tree.

He remained there all night, listening to the sound of the guns and ever praying, praying that his useless life would be spared.

As dawn began to break, he could discern little dark objects protruding from the ground all about him. Curiosity mastered his fear and he crawled to one of the objects, and there, in the uncertain light, he read on a little wooden cross:

"Pte. H. S. Wheaton, No. 1670, 1st London Regt. R. F. Killed in action, April 25, 1916. R. I. P." (Rest in Peace).

When it dawned on him that he had been hiding all night in a cemetery, his reason seemed to leave him, and a mad desire to be free from it all made him rush madly away, falling over little wooden crosses, smashing some and trampling others under his feet.

In his flight, he came to an old French dugout, half caved in, and partially filled with slimy and filthy water.

Like a fox being chased by the hounds, he ducked into this hole, and threw himself on a pile of old empty sandbags, wet and mildewed. Then—unconsciousness.

On the next day, he came to; far distant voices sounded in his ears. Opening his eyes, in the entrance of the dugout he saw a Corporal and two men with fixed bayonets.

The Corporal was addressing him:

"Get up, you white-livered blighter! Curse you and the day you ever joined "D" Company, spoiling their fine record! It'll be you up against the wall, and a good job too. Get a hold of him, men, and if he makes a break, give him the bayonet, and send it home, the cowardly sneak. Come on, you, move, we've been looking for you long enough."

Lloyd, trembling and weakened by his long fast, tottered out, assisted by a soldier on each side of him.

They took him before the Captain, but could get nothing out of him but:

"For God's sake, sir, don't have me shot, don't have me shot!"

The Captain, utterly disgusted with him, sent him under escort to Division Headquarters for trial by court-martial, charged with desertion under fire.

They shoot deserters in France.

During his trial, Lloyd sat as one dazed, and could put nothing forward in his defence, only an occasional "Don't have me shot!"

His sentence was passed: "To be shot at 3:38 o'clock on the morning of May 18, 1916." This meant that he had only one more day to live.

He did not realize the awfulness of his sentence, his brain seemed paralyzed. He knew nothing of his trip, under guard, in a motor lorry to the sand-bagged guardroom in the village, where he was dumped on the floor and left, while a sentry with a fixed bayonet paced up and down in front of the entrance.

Bully beef, water, and biscuits were left beside him for his supper.

The sentry, seeing that he ate nothing, came inside and shook him by the shoulder, saying in a kind voice:

"Cheero, laddie, better eat something. You'll feel better. Don't give up hope. You'll be pardoned before morning. I know the way they run these things. They're only trying to scare you, that's all. Come now, that's a good lad, eat something. It'll make the world look different to you."

The good-hearted sentry knew he was lying

about the pardon. He knew nothing short of a miracle could save the poor lad.

Lloyd listened eagerly to his sentry's words, and believed them. A look of hope came into his eyes, and he ravenously ate the meal beside him.

In about an hour's time, the Chaplain came to see him, but Lloyd would have none of him. He wanted no parson; he was to be pardoned.

The artillery behind the lines suddenly opened up with everything they had. An intense bombardment of the enemy's lines had commenced. The roar of the guns was deafening. Lloyd's fears came back with a rush, and he cowered on the earthen floor with his hands over his face.

The sentry, seeing his position, came in and tried to cheer him by talking to him:

"Never mind them guns, boy, they won't hurt you. They are ours. We are giving the 'Boches' a dose of their own medicine. Our boys are going over the top at dawn of the morning to take their trenches. We'll give 'em a taste of cold steel with their sausages and beer. You just sit tight now until they relieve you. I'll have to go now, lad, as it's nearly time for my relief, and I don't want them to see me a-talkin' with you. So long, laddie, cheero."

With this, the sentry resumed the pacing of his post. In about ten minutes' time he was relieved, and a "D" Company man took his place.

Looking into the guardhouse, the sentry noticed the cowering attitude of Lloyd, and, with a sneer, said to him:

"Instead of whimpering in that corner, you ought to be saying your prayers. It's bally conscripts like you what's spoilin' our record. We've been out here nigh onto eighteen months, and you're the first man to desert his post. The whole Battalion is laughin' and pokin' fun at 'D' Company, bad luck to you! but you won't get another chance to disgrace us. They'll put your lights out in the mornin'."

After listening to this tirade, Lloyd, in a faltering voice, asked: "They are not going to shoot me, are they? Why, the other sentry said they'd pardon me. For God's sake—don't tell me I'm to be shot!" and his voice died away in a sob.

"Of course, they're going to shoot you. The other sentry was jest a-kiddin' you. Jest like old Smith. Always a-tryin' to cheer some one. You ain't got no more chance o' bein' pardoned than I have of gettin' to be Colonel of my 'Batt.'"

When the fact that all hope was gone finally

entered Lloyd's brain, a calm seemed to settle
over him, and rising to his knees, with his arms
stretched out to heaven, he prayed, and all of his
soul entered into the prayer:

"Oh, good and merciful God, give me strength
to die like a man! Deliver me from this coward's
death. Give me a chance to die like my mates
in the fighting line, to die fighting for my country.
I ask this of thee."

A peace, hitherto unknown, came to him, and
he crouched and cowered no more, but calmly
waited the dawn, ready to go to his death. The
shells were bursting all around the guardroom,
but he hardly noticed them.

While waiting there, the voice of the sentry,
singing in a low tone, came to him. He was
singing the chorus of the popular trench ditty:

"I want to go home, I want to go home.
 I don't want to go to the trenches no more.
 Where the 'whizzbangs' and 'sausages' roar galore.
 Take me over the sea, where the Allemand can't
   get at me.
 Oh my, I don't want to die! I want to go home."

Lloyd listened to the words with a strange
interest, and wondered what kind of a home he

would go to across the Great Divide. It would be the only home he had ever known.

Suddenly there came a great rushing through the air, a blinding flash, a deafening report, and the sandbag walls of the guardroom toppled over, and then—blackness.

When Lloyd recovered consciousness, he was lying on his right side, facing what used to be the entrance of the guardroom. Now, it was only a jumble of rent and torn sandbags. His head seemed bursting. He slowly rose on his elbow, and there in the east the dawn was breaking. But what was that mangled shape lying over there among the sandbags? Slowly dragging himself to it, he saw the body of the sentry. One look was enough to know that he was dead. The soldier's head was missing. The sentry had had his wish gratified. He had "gone home." He was safe at last from the "whizzbangs" and the Allemand.

Like a flash it came to Lloyd that he was free. Free to go "over the top" with his Company. Free to die like a true Briton fighting for his King and Country. A great gladness and warmth came over him. Carefully stepping over the body of the sentry, he started on a mad race down the ruined street of the village, amid the bursting shells, minding them not, dodging through or around hurrying platoons on their way to also go "over the top." Coming to a communication trench he could not get through. It was blocked with laughing, cheering, and cursing soldiers. Climbing out of the trench, he ran wildly along the top, never heeding the rain of machine-gun bullets and shells, not even hearing the shouts of the officers, telling him to get back into the trench. He was going to join his Company who were in the front line. He was going to *fight* with them. He, the despised coward, had come into his own.

While he was racing along, jumping over trenches crowded with soldiers, a ringing cheer broke out all along the front line, and his heart sank. He knew he was too late. His Company had gone over. But still he ran madly. He would catch them. He would die with them.

Meanwhile his Company had gone "over." They, with the other companies had taken the first and second German trenches, and had pushed steadily on to the third line. "D" Company, led by their Captain, the one who had sent Lloyd to Division Headquarters for trial, charged with desertion, had pushed steadily forward until they found themselves far in advance of the rest of the attacking force. "Bombing out" trench after trench, and using their bayonets, they came to a German communication trench, which ended in a blindsap, and then the Captain, and what was left of his men, knew they were in a trap. They would not retire. "D" Company never retired, and they were "D" Company. Right in front of them they could see hundreds of Germans preparing to rush them with bomb and bayonet. They would have some chance if ammunition and bombs could reach them from the rear. Their supply was exhausted, and the men realized it would be a case of dying as bravely as possible, or making a run for it. But "D" Company would not run. It was against their traditions and principles.

The Germans would have to advance across an open space of three to four hundred yards before they could get within bombing distance of the trench, and then it would be all their own way.

Turning to his Company, the Captain said:

"Men, it's a case of going West for us. We are out of ammunition and bombs, and the 'Boches' have us in a trap. They will bomb us out. Our bayonets are useless here. We will have to go over and meet them, and it's a case of thirty to one, so send every thrust home, and die like the men of 'D' Company should. When I give the word, follow me, and up and at them. Give them hell! God, if we only had a machine gun, we could wipe them out! Here they come, get ready, men."

Just as he finished speaking, . the welcome "pup-pup" of a machine gun in their rear rang out, and the front line of the onrushing German seemed to melt away. They wavered, but once again came rushing onward. Down went their second line. The machine gun was taking an awful toll of lives. Then again they tried to advance, but the machine gun mowed them down. Dropping their rifles and bombs, they broke and fled in a wild rush back to their trench, amid the cheers of "D" Company. They were forming again for another attempt, when in the rear of "D" Company came a mighty cheer. The ammunition had arrived and with it a battalion of Scotch to reinforce them. They were saved. The unknown machine gunner had come to the rescue in the nick of time.

With the reinforcements, it was an easy task to take the third German line.

After the attack was over, the Captain and three of his non-commissioned officers, wended their way back to the position where the machine gun had done its deadly work. He wanted to thank the gunner in the name of "D" Company for his magnificent deed. They arrived at the gun, and an awful sight met their eyes.

Lloyd had reached the front line trench, after his Company had left it. A strange company was nimbly crawling up the trench ladders. They were reinforcements going over. They were Scotties, and they made a magnificent sight in their brightly colored kilts and bare knees.

Jumping over the trench, Lloyd raced across "No Man's Land," unheeding the rain of bullets, leaping over dark forms on the ground, some of which lay still, while others called out to him as he speeded past.

He came to the German front line, but it was deserted, except for heaps of dead and wounded —a grim tribute to the work of *his* Company, good old "D" Company. Leaping trenches, and gasping for breath, Lloyd could see right ahead of him *his* Company in a dead-ended sap of a communication trench, and across the open, away in front of them, a mass of Germans preparing for a charge.

Why didn't "D" Company fire on them? Why were they so strangely silent? What were they waiting for? Then he knew—their ammunition was exhausted.

But what was that on his right? A machine gun. Why didn't it open fire and save them? He would make that gun's crew do their duty. Rushing over to the gun, he saw why it had not opened fire. Scattered around its base lay six still forms. They had brought their gun to consolidate the captured position, but a German machine gun had decreed they would never fire again.

Lloyd rushed to the gun, and grasping the traversing handles, trained it on the Germans. He pressed the thumb piece, but only a sharp click was the result. The gun was unloaded. Then he realized his helplessness. He did not know how to load the gun. Oh, why hadn't he attended the machine-gun course in England? He'd been offered the chance, but with a blush of shame he remembered that he had been afraid. The nickname of the machine gunners had frightened him. They were called the "Suicide Club." Now, because of this fear, his Company would be destroyed, the men of "D" Company would have to die, because he, Albert Lloyd, had been afraid of a name. In his shame he cried like a baby. Anyway he could die with them, and, rising to his feet, he stumbled over the body of one of the gunners, who emitted a faint moan. A gleam of hope flashed through him. Perhaps this man could tell him how to load the gun. Stooping over the body, he gently shook it, and the soldier opened his eyes. Seeing Lloyd, he closed them again, and in a faint voice said:

"Get away, you blighter, leave me alone. I don't want any coward around me."

The words cut Lloyd like a knife, but he was desperate. Taking the revolver out of the holster of the dying man, he pressed the cold muzzle to the soldier's head, and replied:

"Yes, it is Lloyd, the coward of Company 'D,' but so help me God, if you don't tell me how to load that gun, I'll put a bullet through your brain!"

A sunny smile came over the countenance of the dying man, and he said in a faint whisper:

"Good old boy! I knew you wouldn't disgrace our Company——"

Lloyd interposed, "For God's sake, if you want to save that Company you are so proud of, tell me how to load that damned gun!"

As if reciting a lesson in school, the soldier replied in a weak, singsong voice: "Insert tag end of belt in feed block, with left hand pull belt left front. Pull crank handle back on roller, let go, and repeat motion. Gun is now loaded. To fire, raise automatic safety latch, and press thumb piece. Gun is now firing. If gun stops, ascertain position of crank handle——"

But Lloyd waited for no more. With wild joy at his heart, he took a belt from one of the ammunition boxes lying beside the gun, and followed the dying man's instructions. Then he pressed the thumb piece, and a burst of fire rewarded his efforts. The gun was working.

Training it on the Germans, he shouted for joy as their front rank went down.

Traversing the gun back and forth along the mass of Germans, he saw them break and run back to the cover of their trench, leaving their dead and wounded behind. He had saved his Company, he, Lloyd, the coward, had "done his bit." Releasing the thumb piece, he looked at the watch on his wrist. He was still alive, and the hands pointed to "3:38," the time set for his death by the court.

"Ping!"—a bullet sang through the air, and

Lloyd fell forward across the gun. A thin trickle of blood ran down his face from a little, black round hole in his forehead.

The sentence of the court had been "duly carried out."

The Captain slowly raised the limp form drooping over the gun, and, wiping the blood from the white face, recognized it as Lloyd, the coward of "D" Company. Reverently covering the face with his handkerchief, he turned to his "non-coms," and in a voice husky with emotion, addressed them:

"Boys, it's Lloyd the deserter. He has redeemed himself, died the death of a hero. Died that his mates might live."

That afternoon, a solemn procession wended its way toward the cemetery. In the front a stretcher was carried by two Sergeants. Across the stretcher the Union Jack was carefully spread. Behind the stretcher came a Captain and forty-three men, all that were left of "D" Company.

Arriving at the cemetery, they halted in front of an open grave. All about them, wooden crosses were broken and trampled into the ground.

A grizzled old Sergeant, noting this destruction,

muttered under his breath: "Curse the cowardly blighter who wrecked those crosses! If I could only get these two hands around his neck, his trip West would be a short one."

The corpse on the stretcher seemed to move, or it might have been the wind blowing the folds of the Union Jack.

CHAPTER XXV

PREPARING FOR THE BIG PUSH

REJOINING Atwell after the execution I had a hard time trying to keep my secret from him. I think I must have lost at least ten pounds worrying over the affair.

Beginning at seven in the evening it was our duty to patrol all communication and front-line trenches, making note of unusual occurrences, and arresting anyone who should, to us, appear to be acting in a suspicious manner. We slept during the day.

Behind the lines there was great activity, supplies and ammunition pouring in, and long columns of troops constantly passing. We were preparing for the big offensive, the forerunner of the Battle of the Somme or "Big Push."

The never-ending stream of men, supplies, ammunition, and guns pouring into the British lines made a mighty spectacle, one that cannot be described. It has to be witnessed with your own eyes to appreciate its vastness.

At our part of the line the influx of supplies never ended. It looked like a huge snake slowly crawling forward, never a hitch or break, a wonderful tribute to the system and efficiency of Great Britain's "contemptible little army" of five millions of men.

Huge fifteen-inch guns snaked along, foot by foot, by powerful steam tractors. Then a long line of "four point five" batteries, each gun drawn by six horses, then a couple of "nine point two" howitzers pulled by immense caterpillar engines.

When one of these caterpillars would pass me with its mighty monster in tow, a flush of pride would mount to my face, because I could plainly read on the name plate, "Made in U. S. A.," and I would remember that if I wore a name plate it would also read, "Made in U. S. A." Then I would stop to think how thin and straggly that mighty stream would be if all the "Made in U. S. A." parts of it were withdrawn.

Then would come hundreds of limbers and "G. S." wagons drawn by sleek, well-fed mules, ridden by sleek, well-fed men, ever smiling, although grimy with sweat and covered with the fine, white dust of the marvellously well-made French roads.

What a discouraging report the German air men must have taken back to their Division Commanders, and this stream is slowly but surely getting bigger and bigger every day, and the pace is always the same. No slower, no faster, but ever onward, ever forward.

Three weeks before the Big Push of July 1st— as the Battle of the Somme has been called— started, exact duplicates of the German trenches were dug about thirty kilos behind our lines. The layout of the trenches were taken from aeroplane photographs submitted by the Royal Flying Corps. The trenches were correct to the foot; they showed dugouts, saps, barbed wire defences, and danger spots.

Battalions that were to go over in the first waves were sent back for three days to study these trenches, engage in practice attacks, and have night maneuvers. Each man was required to make a map of the trenches and familiarize himself with the names and location of the parts his battalion was to attack.

In the American army non-commissioned officers are put through a course of map making or road sketching, and during my six years' service in the United States Cavalry, I had plenty of practice in this work, therefore mapping these trenches was a comparatively easy task for me. Each man had to submit his map to the Company Commander to be passed upon, and I was lucky enough to have mine selected as being sufficiently authentic to use in the attack.

No photographs or maps are allowed to leave France, but in this case it appealed to me as a valuable souvenir of the Great War and I managed to smuggle it through. At this time it carries no military importance as the British lines, I am happy to say, have since been advanced beyond this point, so it has been reproduced in this book without breaking any regulation or cautions of the British Army.

The whole attack was rehearsed and rehearsed until we heartily cursed the one who had conceived the idea.

The trenches were named according to a system which made it very simple for Tommy to find, even in the dark, any point in the German lines.

These imitation trenches, or trench models, were well guarded from observation by numerous allied planes which constantly circled above them.

No German aeroplane could approach within observing distance. A restricted area was maintained and no civilian was allowed within three miles, so we felt sure that we had a great surprise in store for Fritz.

When we took over the front line we received an awful shock. The Germans displayed signboards over the top of their trench showing the names that we had called their trenches. The signs read "Fair," "Fact," "Fate," and "Fancy" and so on, according to the code names on our map. Then to rub it in, they hoisted some more signs which read, "When are you coming over?" or "Come on, we are ready, stupid English."

It is still a mystery to me how they obtained this knowledge. There had been no raids or prisoners taken, so it must have been the work of spies in our own lines.

Three or four days before the Big Push we tried to shatter Fritz's nerves by feint attacks, and partially succeeded as the official reports of July 1st show.

Although we were constantly bombarding their lines day and night, still we fooled the Germans several times. This was accomplished by throwing an intense barrage into his lines,—then using smoke shells we would put a curtain of white smoke across No Man's Land, completely obstructing his view of our trenches, and would raise our curtain of fire as if in an actual attack. All down our trenches the men would shout and cheer, and Fritz would turn loose with machine-gun, rifle, and shrapnel fire, thinking we were coming over.

After three or four of these dummy attacks his nerves must have been near the breaking point.

On June 24, 1916, at 9:40 in the morning our guns opened up, and hell was let loose. The din was terrific, a constant boom-boom-boom in your ear.

At night the sky was a red glare. Our bombardment had lasted about two hours when Fritz started replying. Although we were sending over ten shells to his one, our casualties were heavy. There was a constant stream of stretchers coming out of the communication trenches and burial parties were a common sight.

In the dugouts the noise of the guns almost hurt. You had the same sensation as when riding on the Subway you enter the tube under the river going to Brooklyn—a sort of pressure on the ear drums, and the ground constantly trembling.

The roads behind the trenches were very

dangerous because Boche shrapnel was constantly bursting over them. We avoided these dangerous spots by crossing through open fields.

The destruction in the German lines was awful and I really felt sorry for them because I realized how they must be clicking it.

From our front-line trench, every now and again, we could hear sharp whistle blasts in the German trenches. These blasts were the signals for stretcher bearers, and meant the wounding or killing of some German in the service of his Fatherland.

Atwell and I had a tough time of it, patrolling the different trenches at night, but after awhile got used to it.

My old outfit, the Machine Gun Company, was stationed in huge elephant dugouts about four hundred yards behind the front-line trench—they were in reserve. Occasionally I would stop in their dugout and have a confab with my former mates. Although we tried to be jolly, still, there was a lurking feeling of impending disaster. Each man was wondering, if, after the slogan, "Over the top with the best of luck," had been sounded, would he still be alive or would he be lying "somewhere in France." In an old dilapidated house, the walls of which were scarred with machine-gun bullets, No. 3 section of the Machine Gun Company had its quarters. The Company's cooks prepared the meals in this billet. On the fifth evening of the bombardment a German eight-inch shell registered a direct hit on the billet and wiped out ten men who were asleep in the supposedly bomb-proof cellar. They were buried the next day and I attended the funeral.

CHAPTER XXVI

ALL QUIET (?) ON THE WESTERN FRONT

A T Brigade Headquarters I happened to over-
hear a conversation between our G. O. C.
(General Officer Commanding) and the Divisional
Commander. From this conversation I learned
that we were to bombard the German lines for
eight days, and on the first of July the "Big
Push" was to commence.

In a few days orders were issued to that effect,
and it was common property all along the line.

On the afternoon of the eighth day of our
strafeing, Atwell and I were sitting in the front-
line trench smoking fags and making out our
reports of the previous night's tour of the trenches,
which we had to turn in to headquarters the
following day, when an order was passed down
the trench that Old Pepper requested twenty
volunteers to go over on a trench raid that night
to try and get a few German prisoners for informa-

These were the instructions he gave us:

"Take off your identification disks, strip your uniforms of all numerals, insignia, etc., leave your papers with your captains, because I don't want the Boches to know what regiments are against them as this would be valuable information to them in our attack to-morrow and I don't want any of you to be taken alive. What I want is two prisoners and if I get them I have a way which will make them divulge all necessary information as to their guns. You have your choice of two weapons—you may carry your 'persuaders' or your knuckle knives, and each man will arm himself with four Mills bombs, these to be used only in case of emergency."

A persuader is Tommy's nickname for a club carried by the bombers. It is about two feet long, thin at one end and very thick at the other. The thick end is studded with sharp steel spikes, while through the center of the club there is a nine-inch lead bar, to give it weight and balance. When you get a prisoner all you have to do is just stick this club up in front of him, and believe me, the prisoner's patriotism for *Deutschland ueber Alles* fades away and he very willingly obeys the orders of his captor. If, however, the prisoner gets high-toned and refuses to follow you, simply "persuade" him by first removing his tin hat, and then—well, the use of the lead weight in the persuader is demonstrated, and Tommy looks for another prisoner.

The knuckle knife is a dagger affair, the blade of which is about eight inches long with a heavy steel guard over the grip. This guard is studded with steel projections. At night in a trench, which is only about three to four feet wide, it makes a very handy weapon. One punch in the face generally shatters a man's jaw and you can get him with the knife as he goes down.

Then we had what we called our "come-alongs." These are strands of barbed wire about three feet long, made into a noose at one end; at the other end, the barbs are cut off and Tommy slips his wrist through a loop to get a good grip on the wire. If the prisoner wants to argue the point, why just place the large loop around his neck and no matter if Tommy wishes to return to his trenches at the walk, trot, or gallop, Fritz is perfectly agreeable to maintain Tommy's rate of speed.

We were ordered to black our faces and hands. For this reason: at night, the English and Germans

use what they call star shells, a sort of rocket
affair. These are fired from a large pistol about
twenty inches long, which is held over the sandbag parapet of the trench, and discharged into the
air. These star shells attain a height of about
sixty feet, and a range of from fifty to seventy-
five yards. When they hit the ground they explode,
throwing out a strong calcium light which lights
up the ground in a circle of a radius of between
ten to fifteen yards. They also have a parachute
star shell which, after reaching a height of about
sixty feet, explodes. A parachute unfolds and
slowly floats to the ground, lighting up a large
circle in No Man's Land. The official name of
the star shell is a "Very-light." Very-lights are
used to prevent night surprise attacks on the
trenches. If a star shell falls in front of you, or
between you and the German lines, you are safe
from detection, as the enemy cannot see you
through the bright curtain of light. But if it
falls behind you and, as Tommy says, "you get
into the star shell zone," then the fun begins;
you have to lie flat on your stomach and remain
absolutely motionless until the light of the shell
dies out. This takes anywhere from forty to
seventy seconds. If you haven't time to fall to

the ground you must remain absolutely still in whatever position you were in when the light exploded; it is advisable not to breathe, as Fritz has an eye like an eagle when he thinks you are knocking at his door. When a star shell is burning in Tommy's rear he can hold his breath for a week.

You blacken your face and hands so that the light from the star shells will not reflect on your pale face. In a trench raid there is quite sufficient reason for your face to be pale. If you don't believe me, try it just once.

Then another reason for blacking your face and hands is that, after you have entered the German trench at night, "white face" means Germans, "black face" English. Coming around a traverse you see a white face in front of you. With a prayer and wishing Fritz "the best o' luck," you introduce him to your "persuader" or knuckle knife.

A little later we arrived at the communication trench named Whiskey Street, which led to the fire trench at the point we were to go over the top and out in front.

In our rear were four stretcher bearers and a Corporal of the R. A. M. C. carrying a pouch containing medicines and first-aid appliances. Kind of a grim reminder to us that our expedition was not going to be exactly a picnic. The order of things was reversed. In civilian life the doctors generally come first, with the undertakers tagging in the rear and then the insurance man, but in our case, the undertakers were leading, with the doctors trailing behind, minus the insurance adjuster.

The presence of the R. A. M. C. men did not seem to disturb the raiders, because many a joke, made in an undertone, was passed along the winding column, as to who would be first to take a ride on one of the stretchers. This was generally followed by a wish that, if you were to be the one, the wound would be a "cushy Blighty one."

The stretcher bearers, no doubt, were hoping that, if they did have to carry anyone to the rear, he would be small and light. Perhaps they looked at me when wishing, because I could feel an uncomfortable, boring sensation between my shoulder blades. They got their wish all right.

Going up this trench, about every sixty yards or so we would pass a lonely sentry, who in a whisper would wish us "the best o' luck, mates."

We would blind at him under our breaths; that Jonah phrase to us sounded very ominous.

Without any casualties the minstrel troop arrived in Suicide Ditch, the front-line trench. Previously, a wiring party of the Royal Engineers had cut a lane through our barbed wire to enable us to get out into No Man's Land.

Crawling through this lane, our party of twenty took up an extended-order formation about one yard apart. We had a tap code arranged for our movements while in No Man's Land, because for various reasons it is not safe to carry on a heated conversation a few yards in front of Fritz's lines. The officer was on the right of the line, while I was on the extreme left. Two taps from the right would be passed down the line until I received them, then I would send back one tap. The officer, in receiving this one tap, would know that his order had gone down the whole line, had been understood, and that the party was ready to obey the two-tap signal. Two taps meant that we were to crawl forward slowly—and believe me, very slowly—for five yards, and then halt to await further instructions. Three taps meant, when you arrived within striking distance of the German trench, rush it and inflict as many casualties as possible, secure a couple of prisoners, and then back to your own lines with the speed clutch open. Four taps meant, "I have gotten you into a position from which it is impossible for me to extricate you, so you are on your own."

After getting Tommy into a mess on the western front he is generally told that he is "on his own." This means, "Save your skin in any way possible." Tommy loves to be "on his own" behind the lines, but not during a trench raid.

The star shells from the German lines were falling in front of us, therefore we were safe. After about twenty minutes we entered the star shell zone. A star shell from the German lines fell about five yards in the rear and to the right of me; we hugged the ground and held our breath until it burned out. The smoke from the star shell travelled along the ground and crossed over the middle of our line. Some Tommy sneezed. The smoke had gotten up his nose. We crouched on the ground, cursing the offender under our breath, and waited the volley that generally ensues when the Germans have heard a noise in No Man's Land. Nothing happened. We received two taps and crawled forward slowly for five yards; no doubt the officer believed what Old Pepper had said, "Personally I believe that that part of the German trench is unoccupied." By being careful and remaining motionless when the star shells fell behind us, we reached the German barbed wire without mishap. Then the fun began. I was scared stiff as it is ticklish work cutting your way through wire when about thirty feet in front of you there is a line of Boches looking out into No Man's Land with their rifles lying across the parapet, straining every sense to see or hear what is going on in No Man's Land; because at night, Fritz never knows when a bomb with his name and number on it will come hurtling through the air, aimed in the direction of Berlin. The man on the right, one man in the center, and myself on the extreme left were equipped with wire cutters. These are insulated with soft rubber, not because the German wires are charged with electricity, but to prevent the cutters rubbing against the barbed wire stakes, which are of iron, and making a noise which may warn the inmates of the trench that someone is getting fresh in their front yard. There is only one way to cut a barbed wire without noise and through costly experience Tommy has become an expert in doing this.

You must grasp the wire about two inches from the stake in your right hand and cut between the stake and your hand.

If you cut a wire improperly, a loud twang will ring out on the night air like the snapping of a banjo string. Perhaps this noise can be heard only for fifty or seventy-five yards, but in Tommy's mind it makes a loud noise in Berlin.

We had cut a lane about halfway through the wire when, down the center of our line, twang! went an improperly cut wire. We crouched down, cursing under our breath, trembling all over, our knees lacerated from the strands of the cut barbed wire on the ground, waiting for a challenge and the inevitable volley of rifle fire. Nothing happened. I suppose the fellow who cut the barbed wire improperly was the one who had sneezed about half an hour previously. What we wished him would never make his new year a happy one.

The officer, in my opinion, at the noise of the wire should have given the four-tap signal, which meant, "On your own, get back to your trenches as quickly as possible," but again he must have relied on the spiel that Old Pepper had given us in the dugout, "Personally I believe that that part of the

German trench is unoccupied." Anyway, we got careless, but not so careless that we sang patriotic songs or made any unnecessary noise.

During the intervals of falling star shells we carried on with our wire cutting until at last we succeeded in getting through the German barbed wire. At this point we were only ten feet from the German trenches. If we were discovered, we were like rats in a trap. Our way was cut off unless we ran along the wire to the narrow lane we had cut through. With our hearts in our mouths we waited for the three-tap signal to rush the German trench. Three taps had gotten about halfway down the line when suddenly about ten to twenty German star shells were fired all along the trench and landed in the barbed wire in rear of us, turning night into day and silhouetting us against the wall of light made by the flares. In the glaring light we were confronted by the following unpleasant scene.

All along the German trench, at about three-foot intervals, stood a big Prussian guardsman with his rifle at the aim, and then we found out why we had not been challenged when the man sneezed and the barbed wire had been improperly cut. About three feet in front of the trench they had constructed a single fence of barbed wire and we knew our chances were one thousand to one of returning alive. We could not rush their trench on account of this second defence. Then in front of me the challenge, "Halt," given in English rang out, and one of the finest things I have ever heard on the western front took place.

From the middle of our line some Tommy answered the challenge with, "Aw, go to hell." It must have been the man who had sneezed or who had improperly cut the barbed wire; he wanted to show Fritz that he could die game. Then came the volley. Machine guns were turned loose and several bombs were thrown in our rear. The Boche in front of me was looking down his sight. This fellow might have, under ordinary circumstances, been handsome, but when I viewed him from the front of his rifle he had the goblins of childhood imagination relegated to the shade.

Then came a flash in front of me, the flare of his rifle—and my head seemed to burst. A bullet had hit me on the left side of my face about half an inch from my eye, smashing the cheek bones. I put my hand to my face and fell forward, biting the ground and kicking my feet. I thought I was dying, but do you know, my past life did not unfold before me the way it does in novels.

The blood was streaming down my tunic, and the pain was awful. When I came to I said to myself, "Emp, old boy, you belong in Jersey City and you'd better get back there as quickly as possible."

The bullets were cracking overhead. I crawled a few feet back to the German barbed wire, and in a stooping position, guiding myself by the wire, I went down the line looking for the lane we had cut through. Before reaching this lane I came to a limp form which seemed like a bag of oats hanging over the wire. In the dim light I could see that its hands were blackened, and knew it was the body of one of my mates. I put my hand on his head, the top of which had been blown off by a bomb. My fingers sank into the hole. I pulled my hand back full of blood and brains, then I went crazy with fear and horror and rushed along the wire until I came to our lane. I had just turned down this lane when something inside of me seemed to say, "Look around." I did so; a bullet caught me on the left shoulder. It did not hurt much, just felt as if someone had punched me in the back, and then my left side went numb. My arm was dangling like a rag. I fell forward in a sitting position. But all fear had left me and I was consumed with rage and cursed the German trenches. With my right hand I felt in my tunic for my first-aid or shell dressing. In feeling over my tunic my hand came in contact with one of the bombs which I carried. Gripping it, I pulled the pin out with my teeth and blindly threw it towards the German trench. I must have been out of my head because I was only ten feet from the trench and took a chance of being mangled. If the bomb had failed to go into the trench I would have been blown to bits by the explosion of my own bomb.

By the flare of the explosion of the bomb, which luckily landed in their trench, I saw one big Boche throw up his arms and fall backwards, while his rifle flew into the air. Another one wilted and fell forward across the sandbags— then blackness.

Realizing what a foolhardy and risky thing I had done, I was again seized with a horrible fear. I dragged myself to my feet and ran madly down the lane through the barbed wire, stumbling over cut wires, tearing my uniform, and lacerating my hands and legs. Just as I was about to reach No Man's Land again, that same voice seemed to

say, "Turn around." I did so, when, "crack,"
another bullet caught me, this time in the left
shoulder about one half inch away from the other
wound. Then it was taps for me. The lights
went out.

When I came to I was crouching in a hole in
No Man's Land. This shell hole was about three
feet deep, so that it brought my head a few inches
below the level of the ground. How I reached
this hole I will never know. German "type-
writers" were traversing back and forth in No
Man's Land, the bullets biting the edge of my
shell hole and throwing dirt all over me.

Overhead, shrapnel was bursting. I could hear
the fragments slap the ground. Then I went out
once more. When I came to, everything was
silence and darkness in No Man's Land. I was
soaked with blood and a big flap from the wound
in my cheek was hanging over my mouth. The
blood running from this flap choked me. Out of
the corner of my mouth I would try and blow it
back but it would not move. I reached for my
shell dressing and tried, with one hand, to bandage
my face to prevent the flow. I had an awful horror
of bleeding to death and was getting very faint.
You would have laughed if you had seen my

ludicrous attempts at bandaging with one hand. The pains in my wounded shoulder were awful and I was getting sick at the stomach. I gave up the bandaging stunt as a bad job, and then fainted.

When I came to, hell was let loose. An intense bombardment was on, and on the whole my position was decidedly unpleasant. Then, suddenly, our barrage ceased. The silence almost hurt, but not for long, because Fritz turned loose with shrapnel, machine guns, and rifle fire. Then all along our line came a cheer and our boys came over the top in a charge. The first wave was composed of "Jocks." They were a magnificent sight, kilts flapping in the wind, bare knees showing, and their bayonets glistening. In the first wave that passed my shell hole, one of the "Jocks," an immense fellow, about six feet two inches in height, jumped right over me. On the right and left of me several soldiers in colored kilts were huddled on the ground, then over came the second wave, also "Jocks." One young Scottie, when he came abreast of my shell hole, leaped into the air, his rifle shooting out of his hands, landing about six feet in front of him, bayonet first, and stuck in the ground, the butt trembling. This impressed me greatly.

Right now I can see the butt of that gun trembling. The Scottie made a complete turn in the air, hit the ground, rolling over twice, each time clawing at the earth, and then remained still, about four feet from me, in a sort of sitting position. I called to him, "Are you hurt badly, Jock?" but no answer. He was dead. A dark, red smudge was coming through his tunic right under the heart. The blood ran down his bare knees, making a horrible sight. On his right side he carried his water bottle. I was crazy for a drink and tried to reach this, but for the life of me could not negotiate that four feet. Then I became unconscious. When I woke up I was in an advanced first-aid post. I asked the doctor if we had taken the trench. "We took the trench and the wood beyond, all right," he said, "and you fellows did your bit; but, my lad, that was thirty-six hours ago. You were lying in No Man's Land in that bally hole for a day and a half. It's a wonder you are alive." He also told me that out of the twenty that were in the raiding party, seventeen were killed. The officer died of wounds in crawling back to our trench and I was severely wounded, but one fellow returned without a scratch without any prisoners. No doubt this chap was the one who had sneezed and improperly cut the barbed wire.

In the official communique our trench raid was described as follows:

"All quiet on the Western front, excepting in the neighborhood of Gommecourt Wood, where one of our raiding parties penetrated into the German lines."

It is needless to say that we had no use for our persuaders or come-alongs, as we brought back no prisoners, and until I die Old Pepper's words, "Personally I don't believe that that part of the German trench is occupied," will always come to me when I hear some fellow trying to get away with a fishy statement. I will judge it accordingly.

CHAPTER XXVII

BLIGHTY

FROM this first-aid post, after inoculating me with anti-tetanus serum to prevent lockjaw, I was put into an ambulance and sent to a temporary hospital behind the lines. To reach this hospital we had to go along a road about five miles in length. This road was under shell fire, for now and then a flare would light up the sky,—a tremendous explosion,—and then the road seemed to tremble. We did not mind, though no doubt some of us wished that a shell would hit us and end our misery. Personally, I was not particular. It was nothing but bump, jolt, rattle, and bang.

Several times the driver would turn around and give us a "Cheero, mates, we'll soon be there—" fine fellows, those ambulance drivers, a lot of them go West too.

We gradually drew out of the fire zone and pulled up in front of an immense dugout. Stretcher-bearers carried me down a number of steps and placed me on a white table in a brightly lighted room.

A Sergeant of the Royal Army Medical Corps removed my bandages and cut off my tunic. Then the doctor, with his sleeves rolled up, took charge. He winked at me and I winked back, and then he asked, "How do you feel, smashed up a bit?"

I answered: "I'm all right, but I'd give a quid for a drink of Bass."

He nodded to the Sergeant who disappeared, and I'll be darned if he didn't return with a glass of ale. I could only open my mouth about a quarter of an inch, but I got away with every drop of that ale. It tasted just like Blighty, and that is heaven to Tommy.

The doctor said something to an orderly, the only word I could catch was "chloroform," then they put some kind of an arrangement over my nose and mouth and it was me for dreamland.

When I opened my eyes I was lying on a stretcher, in a low wooden building. Everywhere I looked I saw rows of Tommies on stretchers, some dead to the world, and the rest with fags in their mouths.

The main topic of their conversation was Blighty. Nearly all had a grin on their faces, except those who didn't have enough face left to grin with. I grinned with my right eye, the other was bandaged.

Stretcher-bearers came in and began to carry the Tommies outside. You could hear the chug of the engines in the waiting ambulances.

I was put into a Ford with three others and away we went for an eighteen-mile ride. Keep out of a Ford when you are wounded; insist on walking, it'll pay you.

I was on a bottom stretcher. The lad right across from me was smashed up something horrible.

Right above me was a man from the Royal Irish Rifles, while across from him was a Scotchman.

We had gone about three miles when I heard the death-rattle in the throat of the man opposite. He had gone to rest across the Great Divide. I think at the time I envied him.

The man of the Royal Irish Rifles had had his left foot blown off, the jolting of the ambulance over the rough road had loosened up the bandages on his foot, and had started it bleeding again.

This blood ran down the side of the stretcher and started dripping. I was lying on my back, too weak to move, and the dripping of this blood got me in my unbandaged right eye. I closed my eye and pretty soon could not open the lid; the blood had congealed and closed it, as if it were glued down.

An English girl dressed in khaki was driving the ambulance, while beside her on the seat was a Corporal of the R. A. M. C. They kept up a running conversation about Blighty which almost wrecked my nerves; pretty soon from the stretcher above me, the Irishman became aware of the fact that the bandage from his foot had become loose; it must have pained him horribly, because he yelled in a loud voice:

"If you don't stop this bloody death wagon and fix this damned bandage on my foot, I will get out and walk."

The girl on the seat turned around and in a sympathetic voice asked, "Poor fellow, are you very badly wounded?"

The Irishman, at this question, let out a howl of indignation and answered, "Am I very badly wounded, what bloody cheek; no, I'm not wounded, I've only been kicked by a canary bird."

The ambulance immediately stopped, and the Corporal came to the rear and fixed him up, and also washed out my right eye. I was too weak to thank him, but it was a great relief. Then I must have become unconscious, because when I regained my senses, the ambulance was at a standstill, and my stretcher was being removed from it.

It was night, lanterns were flashing here and there, and I could see stretcher-bearers hurrying to and fro. Then I was carried into a hospital train.

The inside of this train looked like heaven to me, just pure white, and we met our first Red Cross nurses; we thought they were angels. And they were.

Nice little soft bunks and clean, white sheets.

A Red Cross nurse sat beside me during the whole ride which lasted three hours. She was holding my wrist; I thought I had made a hit, and tried to tell her how I got wounded, but she would put her finger to her lips and say, "Yes, I know, but you mustn't talk now, try to go to sleep, it'll do you good, doctor's orders." Later on I learned that she was taking my pulse every few minutes, as I was very weak from the loss of blood and they expected me to snuff it, but I didn't.

From the train we went into ambulances for a short ride to the hospital ship *Panama*. Another palace and more angels. I don't remember the trip across the channel.

I opened my eyes; I was being carried on a stretcher through lanes of people, some cheering, some waving flags, and others crying. The flags were Union Jacks, I was in Southampton. Blighty at last. My stretcher was strewn with flowers, cigarettes, and chocolates. Tears started to run down my cheek from my good eye. I like a booby was crying, can you beat it?

Then into another hospital train, a five-hour ride to Paignton, another ambulance ride, and then I was carried into Munsey Ward of the American Women's War Hospital and put into a real bed.

This real bed was too much for my unstrung nerves and I fainted.

When I came to, a pretty Red Cross nurse was bending over me, bathing my forehead with cold water, then she left and the ward orderly placed a screen around my bed, and gave me a much-needed bath and clean pajamas. Then the screen was removed and a bowl of steaming soup was given me. It tasted delicious.

Before finishing my soup the nurse came back to ask me my name and number. She put this information down in a little book and then asked:

"Where do you come from?" I answered:

"From the big town behind the Statue of Liberty"; upon hearing this she started jumping up and down, clapping her hands, and calling out to three nurses across the ward:

"Come here, girls—at last we have got a real live Yankee with us."

They came over and besieged me with questions, until the doctor arrived. Upon learning that I was an American he almost crushed my hand in his grip of welcome. They also were Americans, and were glad to see me.

The doctor very tenderly removed my bandages and told me, after viewing my wounds, that he would have to take me to the operating theater immediately. Personally I didn't care what was done with me.

In a few minutes, four orderlies who looked like undertakers dressed in white, brought a stretcher to my bed and placing me on it carried me out of the ward, across a courtyard to the operating room or "pictures," as Tommy calls it.

I don't remember having the anæsthetic applied.

After the Trench Raid.

When I came to I was again lying in a bed in Munsey Ward. One of the nurses had draped a large American flag over the head of the bed, and clasped in my hand was a smaller flag, and it made me feel good all over, to again see the "Stars and Stripes."

At that time I wondered when the boys in the trenches would see the emblem of the "land of the free and the home of the brave" beside them, doing its bit in this great war of civilization.

My wounds were very painful, and several times at night I would dream that myriads of khaki-clothed figures would pass my bed and each would stop, bend over me, and whisper, "The best of luck, mate."

Soaked with perspiration I would awake with a cry, and the night nurse would come over and hold my hand. This awakening got to be a habit with me, until that particular nurse was transferred to another ward.

In three weeks' time, owing to the careful treatment received, I was able to sit up and get my bearings. Our ward contained seventy-five patients, ninety per cent. of which were surgical cases. At the head of each bed hung a temperature chart and diagnosis sheet. Across this sheet would be

written "G. S. W." or "S. W." the former meaning
Gun Shot Wound and the latter Shell Wound.
The "S. W." predominated, especially among the
Royal Field Artillery and Royal Engineers.

About forty different regiments were represented
and many arguments ensued as to the respective
fighting ability of each regiment. The rivalry
was wonderful. A Jock arguing with an Irishman,
then a strong Cockney accent would butt in in favor
of a London Regiment. Before long a Welshman,
followed by a member of a Yorkshire regiment, and,
perhaps, a Canadian intrude themselves and the
argument waxes loud and furious. The patients
in the beds start howling for them to settle their
dispute outside and the ward is in an uproar.
The head sister comes along and with a wave of the
hand completely routs the doughty warriors and
again silence reigns supreme.

Wednesday and Sunday of each week were
visiting days and were looked forward to by the
men, because they meant parcels containing fruit,
sweets, or fags. When a patient had a regular
visitor, he was generally kept well supplied with
these delicacies. Great jealousy is shown among
the men as to their visitors and many word wars
ensue after the visitors leave.

When a man is sent to a convalescent home, he generally turns over his steady visitor to the man in the next bed.

Most visitors have autograph albums and bore Tommy to death by asking him to write the particulars of his wounding in same. Several Tommies try to duck this unpleasant job by telling the visitor that he cannot write, but this never phases the owner of the album; he or she, generally she, offers to write it for him and Tommy is stung into telling his experiences.

The questions asked Tommy by visitors would make a clever joke book to a military man.

Some kindly looking old lady will stop at your bed and in a sympathetic voice address you: "You poor boy, wounded by those terrible Germans. You must be suffering frightful pain. A bullet did you say? Well, tell me, I have always wanted to know, did it hurt worse going in or coming out?"

Tommy generally replies that he did not stop to figure it out when he was hit.

One very nice-looking, over enthusiastic young thing, stopped at my bed and asked, "What wounded you in the face?"

In a polite but bored tone I answered, "A rifle bullet."

With a look of disdain she passed to the next bed, first ejaculating, "Oh! only a bullet? I thought it was a shell." Why she should think a shell wound was more of a distinction beats me. I don't see a whole lot of difference myself.

The American Women's War Hospital was a heaven for wounded men. They were allowed every privilege possible conducive with the rules and military discipline. The only fault was that the men's passes were restricted. To get a pass required an act of Parliament. Tommy tried many tricks to get out, but the Commandant, an old Boer War officer, was wise to them all, and it took a new and clever ruse to make him affix his signature to the coveted slip of paper.

As soon as it would get dark many a patient climbed over the wall and went "on his own," regardless of many signs staring him in the face, "Out of bounds for patients." Generally the nurses were looking the other way when one of these night raids started. I hope this information will get none of them into trouble, but I cannot resist the temptation to let the Commandant know that occasionally we put it over on him.

One afternoon I received a note, through our underground channel, from my female visitor,

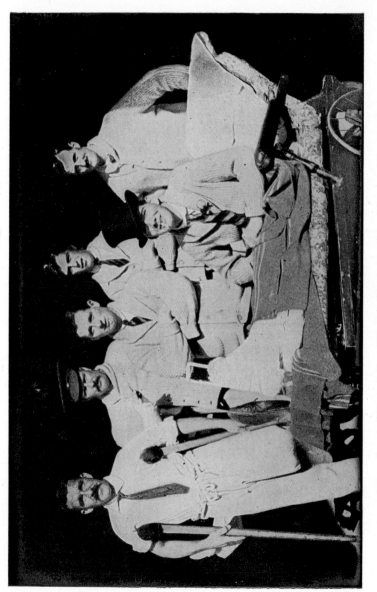

A "Downhearted" Bunch from Munsey Ward, American Women's War Hospital.

asking me to attend a party at her house that night. I answered that she could expect me and to meet me at a certain place on the road well known by all patients, and some visitors, as "Over the wall." I told her I would be on hand at seven-thirty.

About seven-fifteen I sneaked my overcoat and cap out of the ward and hid it in the bushes. Then I told the nurse, a particular friend of mine, that I was going for a walk in the rose garden. She winked and I knew that everything was all right on her end.

Going out of the ward, I slipped into the bushes and made for the wall. It was dark as pitch and I was groping through the underbrush, when suddenly I stepped into space and felt myself rushing downward, a horrible bump, and blackness. When I came to, my wounded shoulder was hurting horribly. I was lying against a circular wall of bricks, dripping with moisture, and far away I could hear the trickling of water. I had in the darkness fallen into an old disused well. But why wasn't I wet? According to all rules I should have been drowned. Perhaps I was and didn't know it.

As the shock of my sudden stop gradually wore

off, it came to me that I was lying on a ledge and that the least movement on my part would precipitate me to the bottom of the well.

I struck a match. In its faint glare I saw that I was lying in a circular hole about twelve feet deep,—the well had been filled in! The dripping I had heard came from a water pipe over on my right.

With my wounded shoulder it was impossible to shinny up the pipe. I could not yell for help, because the rescuer would want to know how the accident happened, and I would be haled before the Commandant on charges. I just had to grin and bear it with the forlorn hope that one of the returning night raiders would pass and I could give him our usual signal of "siss-s-s-s" which would bring him to the rescue.

Every half-hour I could hear the clock in the village strike, each stroke bringing forth a muffled volley of curses on the man who had dug the well.

After two hours, I heard two men talking in low voices. I recognized Corporal Cook, an ardent "night raider." He heard my "siss-s-s-s" and came to the edge of the hole. I explained my predicament and amid a lot of impertinent remarks, which at the time I did not resent, I was soon fished out.

Taking off our boots we sneaked into the ward. I was sitting on my bed in the dark, just starting to undress, when the man next to me, "Ginger" Phillips, whispered, "'Op it, Yank, 'ere comes the matron."

I immediately got under the covers and feigned sleep. The matron stood talking in low tones to the night nurse and I fell asleep.

When I awoke in the morning the night sister, an American, was bending over me. An awful sight met my eyes. The coverlet on the bed and the sheets were a mass of mud and green slime. She was a good sport all right and hustled to get clean clothes and sheets so that no one would get wise, but "on her own" she gave me a good tongue lashing but did not report me. One of the Canadians in the ward described her as being "A Jake of a good fellow."

Next visiting day I had an awful time explaining to my visitor why I had not met her at the appointed time and place.

And for a week every time I passed a patient he would call, "*Well*, *well*, here's the Yank. Hope you are feeling *well*, old top."

The surgeon in our ward was an American, a Harvard Unit man, named Frost. We nicknamed him "Jack Frost." He was loved by all. If a Tommy was to be cut up he had no objection to undergoing the operation if "Jack Frost" was to wield the knife. Their confidence in him was pathetic. He was the best sport I have ever met.

One Saturday morning the Commandant and some "high up" officers were inspecting the ward, when one of the patients who had been wounded in the head by a bit of shrapnel, fell on the floor in a fit. They brought him round, and then looked for the ward orderly to carry the patient back to his bed at the other end of the ward. The orderly was nowhere to be found—like our policemen, they never are when needed. The officers were at a loss how to get Palmer into his bed. Dr. Frost was fidgeting around in a nervous manner, when suddenly with a muffled "damn" and a few other qualifying adjectives, he stooped down and took the man in his arms like a baby,—he was no feather either,—and staggered down the ward with him, put him in bed, and undressed him. A low murmur of approval came from the patients. Dr. Frost got very red and as soon as he had finished undressing Palmer, hurriedly left the ward.

The wound in my face had almost healed and I was a horrible-looking sight—the left cheek twisted into a knot, the eye pulled down, and my mouth pointing in a north by northwest direction. I was very down-hearted and could imagine myself during the rest of my life being shunned by all on account of the repulsive scar.

Dr. Frost arranged for me to go to the Cambridge Military Hospital at Aldershot for a special operation to try and make the scar presentable.

I arrived at the hospital and got an awful shock. The food was poor and the discipline abnormally strict. No patient was allowed to sit on his bed, and smoking was permitted only at certain designated hours. The face specialist did nothing for me except to look at the wound. I made application for a transfer back to Paignton, offering to pay my transportation. This offer was accepted, and after two weeks' absence, once again I arrived in Munsey Ward, all hope gone.

The next day after my return, Dr. Frost stopped at my bed and said: "Well, Empey, if you want me to try and see what I can do with that scar, I'll do it, but you are taking an awful chance."

I answered: "Well, Doctor, Steve Brodie took a chance; he hails from New York and so do I."

Two days after the undertaker squad carried me to the operating room or "pictures," as we called them because of the funny films we see under ether, and the operation was performed. It was a wonderul piece of surgery and a marvelous success. From now on that doctor can have my shirt.

More than once some poor soldier has been brought into the ward in a dying condition, resulting from loss of blood and exhaustion caused by his long journey from the trenches. After an examination the doctor announces that the only thing that will save him is a transfusion of blood. Where is the blood to come from? He does not have to wait long for an answer,—several Tommies immediately volunteer their blood for their mate. Three or four are accepted; a blood test is made, and next day the transfusion takes place and there is another pale face in the ward.

Whenever bone is needed for some special operation, there are always men willing to give some,—a leg if necessary to save some mangled mate from being crippled for life. More than one man will go through life with another man's blood running through his veins, or a piece of his rib or his shinbone in his own anatomy. Sometimes he never even knows the name of his benefactor.

The spirit of sacrifice is wonderful.

For all the suffering caused this war is a blessing to England—it has made new men of her sons; has welded all classes into one glorious whole.

And I can't help saying that the doctors, sisters, and nurses in the English hospitals, are angels on earth. I love them all and can never repay the care and kindness shown to me. For the rest of my life the Red Cross will be to me the symbol of Faith, Hope, and Charity.

After four months in the hospital, I went before an examining board and was discharged from the service of his Britannic Majesty as " physically unfit for further war service."

After my discharge I engaged passage on the American liner, *New York*, and after a stormy trip across the Atlantic, one momentous day, in the haze of early dawn I saw the Statue of Liberty looming over the port rail, and I wondered if ever again I would go "over the top with the best of luck and give them hell."

And even then, though it may seem strange, I was really sorry not to be back in the trenches with my mates. War is not a pink tea but in a worthwhile cause like ours, mud, rats, cooties, shells, wounds, or death itself, are far outweighed by the deep sense of satisfaction felt by the man who does his bit.

There is one thing which my experience taught me that might help the boy who may have to go. It is this—anticipation is far worse than realization. In civil life a man stands in awe of the man above him, wonders how he could ever fill his job. When the time comes he rises to the occasion, is up and at it, and is surprised to find how much more easily than he anticipated he fills his responsibilities. It is really so "out there."

He has nerve for the hardships; the interest of the work grips him; he finds relief in the fun and comradeship of the trenches and wins that best sort of happiness that comes with duty done.

"TOMMY'S DICTIONARY OF THE TRENCHES"

In this so-called dictionary I have tried to list most of the pet terms and slangy definitions, which Tommy Atkins uses a thousand times a day as he is serving in France. I have gathered them as I lived with him in the trenches and rest billets, and later in the hospitals in England where I met men from all parts of the line.

The definitions are not official, of course. Tommy is not a sentimental sort of animal so some of his definitions are not exactly complimentary, but he is not cynical and does not mean to offend any-one higher up. It is just a sort of "ragging" or "kidding," as the American would say, that helps him pass the time away.

SLANG TERMS, SAYINGS, PHRASES, ETC.

A

"About turn." A military command similar to "About face" or "To the rear, march." Tommy's nickname for Hebu-terne, a point on the British line.

Adjutant. The name given to an officer who helps the Colonel do nothing. He rides a horse and you see him at guard mounting and battalion parade.

A. D. M. S. Assistant Director of Medical Service. Have never seen him but he is supposed to help the D. M. S. and pass on cases where Tommy is posted as "unfit for trench service."

Aërial Torpedo. A kind of trench mortar shell, guaranteed by the makers to break up Fritz's supper of sausages and beer, even though said supper is in a dugout thirty feet down. Sometimes it lives up to its reputation.

Alarm. A signal given in the trenches that the enemy is about to attack, frequently false. It is mainly used to break up Tommy's dreams of home.

"All around traverse." A machine gun so placed that its fire can be turned in any direction.

Allemand. A French term meaning "German." Tommy uses it because he thinks it is a swear word.

Allotment. A certain sum Tommy allows to his family.

Allumettes. French term for what they sell to Tommy as matches, the sulphurous fumes from which have been known to "gas" a whole platoon.

"Ammo." Rifle ammunition. Used to add weight to Tommy's belt. He carries 120 rounds, at all times, except when he buries it under the straw in his billet before going on a route march. In the trenches he expends it in the direction of Berlin.

Ammo Depot. A place where ammunition is stored. It is especially useful in making enemy airmen waste bombs trying to hit it.

Ammonal. A high explosive used in the Mills bomb. The Germans are more able than Tommy to discourse on its effects.

"Any complaints." A useless question asked by an inspecting officer when he makes the rounds of billets or Tommy's meals. A complaining Tommy generally lands on the crime sheet. It is only recruits who complain; the old men just sigh with disgust.

A. O. C. Army Ordnance Corps. A department which deals out supplies to the troops. Its chief asset is the returning of requisitions because a comma is misplaced.

A. P. M. Assistant Provost Marshal. An officer at the head of the Military Police. His headquarters are generally out of reach of the enemy's guns. His chief duties are to ride around in a motor car and wear a red band around his cap.

"Après la Guerre." "After the war." Tommy's definition of Heaven.

A. S. C. Army Service Corps, or Army Safety Corps as Tommy calls it. The members of which bring up supplies to the rear of the line.

B

"Back o' the line." Any place behind the firing line out of range of enemy guns.

Baler. A scoop affair for baling out water from the trenches and dugouts. As the trenches generally drain the surrounding landscape, the sun has to be appealed to before the job is completed.

Bantams. Men under the standard army height of 5 ft. 3 in. They are in a separate organization called "The Bantam Battalion," and although undersized have the opinion that they can lick the whole German Army.

Barbed Wire. A lot of prickly wire entwined around stakes driven in front of the trenches. This obstruction is supposed to prevent the Germans from taking lodgings in your dugouts. It also affords the enemy artillery rare sport trying to blow it up.

"Barndook." Tommy's nickname for his rifle. He uses it because it is harder to say and spell than "rifle."

Barrage. Concentrated shell-fire on a sector of the German line. In the early days of the war, when ammunition was defective, it often landed on Tommy himself.

Barricade. An obstruction of sandbags to impede the enemy's traffic into your trench. You build it up and he promptly knocks it down, so what's the use.

"Bashed in." Smashed by a shell. Generally applied to a trench or dugout.

Batman. A man who volunteers to clean a non-commissioned officer's buttons but who never volunteers for a trench raid. He ranks next to a worm.

Bayonet. A sort of knife-like contrivance which fits on the end of your rifle. The Government issues it to stab Germans with. Tommy uses it to toast bread.

"Big Boys." Large guns, generally eight inch or above.

"Big Push." "The Battle of the Somme." He often calls it "The First of July," the date on which it started.

" Big Stuff." Large shells, eight inch or over.

" Big Willie." Tommy's term for his personal friend, the Kaiser.

Billet. Sometimes a regular house but generally a stable where Tommy sleeps while behind the lines. It is generally located near a large manure pile. Most billets have numerous entrances—one for Tommy and the rest for rain, rats, wind, and shells.

Billet Guard. Three men and a corporal who are posted to guard the billets of soldiers. They do this until the orderly officer has made his rounds at night, then they go to sleep.

Biscuit. A concoction of flour and water, baked until very hard. Its original use was for building purposes, but Tommy is supposed to eat it. Tommy is no coward but he balks at this. Biscuits make excellent fuel, and give no smoke.

Bivouac. A term given by Tommy to a sort of tent made out of waterproof sheets.

Blastine. A high explosive which promotes Kultur in the German lines.

Blighty. An East Indian term meaning "over the seas." Tommy has adopted it as a synonym for home. He tries numerous ways of reaching Blighty, but the "powers that be" are wise to all of his attempts, so he generally fails.

" Blighty One." A wound serious enough to send Tommy to England.

B. M. G. C. Brigade Machine Gun Company, composed of Vickers machine gunners. They always put their packs on a limber or small wagon while route marching, which fact greatly arouses the jealousy of Tommy.

" Body Snatcher." Tommy's term for a sniper.

Bomb. An infernal device filled with high explosive which you throw at the Germans. Its chief delight is to explode before it leaves your hand.

Bomb Store. A place where bombs are kept, built so the enemy cannot locate them with his fire. For that matter, Tommy can't either when he needs them.

Bombing Post. A sort of trench or sap running from your front line to within a few yards of the enemy's trench. It is occupied by bomb throwers who would like to sign an agreement with the Germans for neither side to throw bombs.

Brag. A card game similar to poker at which every player quits a loser and no one wins, that is, according to the statements of the several players.

Brazier. A sheet iron pot punched full of holes in which a fire is built. It is used to keep Tommy warm in his dugout, until he becomes unconscious from its smoke and fumes. He calls it a "fire bucket."

Brigade Guard. Several men who are detailed to guard Brigade Headquarters. They don't go to sleep.

B. S. M. Battalion Sergeant-Major. The highest ranking non-commissioned officer in the battalion. A constant dread to Tommy when he has forgotten to polish his buttons or dubbin his boots.

Bully Beef. A kind of corned beef with tin round it. The unopened cans make excellent walls for dugouts.

Burm. A narrow ledge cut along the walls of a trench to prevent earth from caving in. "Burm" to Tommy is a cuss word, because he has to "go over the top" at night to construct it.

"Busted." Term applied when a non-commissioned officer is reduced by court-martial.

Button Stick. A contrivance made of brass ten inches long which slides over the buttons and protects the tunic in cleaning.

C

" Called to the colors." A man on reserve who has been ordered to report for service.

" Camel Corps." Tommy's nickname for the Infantry because they look like overloaded camels, and probably because they also go eight days, and longer, without a drink, that is, of the *real stuff*.

Candle. A piece of wick surrounded by wax or tallow used for lighting purposes. One candle among six men is the general issue.

Canister. A German trench mortar shell filled with scraps of iron and nails. Tommy really has a great contempt for this little token of German affection and he uses the nails to hang his equipment on in the dugouts.

Canteen. A mess tin issued to Tommy, who, after dinner, generally forgets to wash it, and pinches his mates for tea in the evening.

"**Carry on.**" Resume. Keep on with what you are doing. Go ahead.

"**Carrying in.**" Machine gunners' term for taking guns, ammunition, etc., into front-line trench.

Caterpillar. Is not a bug, but the name given to a powerful engine used to haul the big guns over rough roads.

C. C. S. Casualty Clearing Station. A place where the doctors draw lots to see if Tommy is badly wounded enough to be sent to Blighty.

Chalk Pit. A white spot on a painted landscape used at the Machine Gunners' School to train would-be gunners in picking out distinctive objects in landscapes and guessing ranges.

Challenge. A question, "Who goes there?" thrown at an unknown moving object by a sentry in the darkness, who hopes that said moving object will answer, "Friend."

Char. A black poisonous brew which Tommy calls tea.

"**Chevaux-de-frise.**" Barbed-wire defenses against cavalry.

"**Chucking his weight about.**" Self-important. Generally applied to a newly promoted non-commissioned officer or a recruit airing his knowledge.

Chum. An endearing word used by Tommy to his mate when he wants to borrow something or have a favor done.

"**Clicked it.**" Got killed; up against it; wounded.

"**Clock.**" "Trench" for the face.

"**Coal Box.**" The nickname for a high explosive German shell fired from a 5.9 howitzer which emits a heavy black smoke and makes Tommy's hair stand on end.

Coal Fatigue. A detail on which Tommy has to ride in a limber and fill two sacks with coal. It takes him exactly four hours to do this. He always misses morning parade, but manages to get back in time for dinner.

"**Cole.**" Tommy's nickname for a penny. It buys one glass of French beer.

"**Coming it.**" Trying to "put something over."

"**Coming the acid.**" Boasting; lying about something.

Communication Trench. A zigzag ditch leading from the rear to the front-line trench, through which reinforcements, reliefs, ammunition, and rations are brought up. Its real use is to teach Tommy how to swear and how to wade through mud up to his knees.

Communique. An official report which is published daily by the different warring governments for the purpose of kidding the public. They don't kid Tommy.

Company Stores. The Quartermaster-Sergeant's headquarters where stores are kept. A general hang-out for batmen, officers' servants, and N. C. O.'s.

"Compray." Tommy's French for "Do you understand?" Universally used in the trenches.

Conscript. A man who tried to wait until the war was over before volunteering for the army, but was balked by the Government.

"Consolidate captured line." Digging in or preparing a captured position for defence against a counter-attack.

Convalescence. Six weeks' rest allotted to a wounded Tommy. During this time the Government is planning where they will send Tommy to be wounded a second time.

C. of E. Church of England. This is stamped on Tommy's identification disk. He has to attend church parade whether or not he wants to go to Heaven.

Cook. A soldier detailed to spoil Tommy's rations. He is generally picked because he was a blacksmith in civil life.

Cooties. Unwelcome inhabitants of Tommy's shirt.

Counter Attack. A disagreeable habit of the enemy which makes Tommy realize that after capturing a position the hardest work is to hold it.

Covering Party. A number of men detailed to lie down in front of a working party while "out in front" to prevent surprise and capture by German patrols. Tommy loves this job, I don't think!

Crater. A large circular hole in the ground made by the explosion of a mine. According to Official Communiques, Tommy always occupies a crater with great credit to himself. But sometimes the Germans get there first.

"Cricket ball." The name given to a bomb the shape and size of a cricket ball. Tommy does not use it to play cricket with.

Crime Sheet. A useless piece of paper on which is kept a record of Tommy's misdemeanors.

"Crump." A name given by Tommy to a high explosive German shell which when it bursts makes a "Cru-mp" sort of noise.

C. S. M. Company Sergeant-Major, the head non-commissioned officer of a company, whose chief duty is to wear a crown on his arm, a couple of Boer War ribbons on his chest, and to put Tommy's name and number on the crime sheet.

"Curtain fire." A term applied by the artillery to a wall of shell fire on the enemy communication trenches, to prevent the bringing up of men and supplies, and also to keep our own front lines from wavering. But somehow or other men and supplies manage to leak through it.

"Cushy." Easy; comfortable; "pretty soft."

D

D. A. C. Divisional Ammunition Column. A collection of men, horses, and limbers, which supplies ammunition for the line and keeps Tommy awake, while in billets, with their infernal noise. They are like owls—always working at night.

D. C. M. Distinguished Conduct Medal. A piece of bronze which a soldier gets for being foolish.

D. C. P. Divisional Concert Party. An aggregation of would-be actors who inflict their talents on Tommy at half a franc per head.

Defaulter. Not an absconding cashier, but a Tommy who has been sentenced to extra pack drill for breathing while on parade or doing some other little thing like that.

"Dekko." To look; a look at something.

Detonator. A contrivance in a bomb containing fulminate of mercury, which, ignited by a fuse, explodes the charge.

"Der uffs." "Deux œufs." Tommy's French for "two eggs."

"Dial." Another term of Tommy's for his map, or face.

"Digging in." Digging trenches and dugouts in a captured position.

Digging Party. A detail of men told off to dig trenches, graves, or dugouts. Tommy is not particular as to what he has to dig; it's the actual *digging* he objects to.

"Dinner up." Dinner is ready.

Divisional Band. Another devilish aggregation which wastes most of its time in practising and polishing its instruments.

Dixie. An iron pot with two handles on it in which Tommy's meals are cooked. Its real efficiency lies in the fact that when carrying it, your puttees absorb all the black grease on its sides.

"Doing them in." Killing them. Cutting up a body of German troops.

Donkey. An army mule. An animal for which Tommy has the greatest respect. He never pets or in any way becomes familiar with said mule.

Draft. A contingent of new men sent as reinforcements for the trenches. Tommy takes special delight in scaring these men with tales of his own experiences which he never had.

Draftman. A member of a draft who listens to *and believes* Tommy's weird tales of trench warfare.

Dressing Station. A medical post where Tommy gets his wounds attended to, if he is lucky enough to get wounded. He is "lucky," because a wound means Blighty.

"Drill order." Rifle, belt, bayonet, and respirator.

Dry Canteen. An army store where Tommy may buy cigarettes, chocolate, and tinned fruit, that is, if he has any money.

D. S. O. Distinguished Service Order. Another piece of metal issued to officers for being brave. Tommy says it is mostly won in dugouts and calls it a "Dugout Service Order."

Dubbin. A grease for boots.

Dud. A German shell or bomb which has not exploded on account of a defective fuse. Tommy is a great souvenir collector so he gathers these "duds." Sometimes when he tries to unscrew the nose-cap it sticks. Then in his hurry to confiscate it before an officer appears he doesn't hammer it just right—and the printer of the casualty list has to use a little more type.

Dugout. A deep hole in the trenches dug by the Royal Engineer Corps; supposed to be shell proof. It is, until a shell hits it. Rat and Tommy find it an excellent habitation in which to contract rheumatism.

Dump. An uncovered spot where trench tools and supplies are placed. It is uncovered so that these will become rusty and worthless from the elements. This so that the contractors at home won't starve.

"Du pan." Tommy's French for bread.

E

Efficiency Pay. Extra pay allowed by the Government for long service. Tommy is very efficient if he manages to get it from the Government.

Eighteen-Pounder. One of our guns which fires an eighteen-pound shell, used for destroying German barbed wire previous to an attack. If it does its duty you bet Tommy is grateful to the eighteen-pounders.

Elephant Dugout. A large, safe, and roomy dugout, braced by heavy steel ribs or girders.

Emplacement. A position made of earth or sandbags from which a machine gun is fired. It is supposed to be invisible to the enemy. They generally blow it up in the course of a couple of days, just by luck, of course.

Entrenching Tool. A spade-like tool for digging hasty entrenchments. It takes about a week to dig a decent hole with it, so "hasty" must have another meaning.

"Equipment on." Put on equipment for drill or parade.

Escort. A guard of soldiers who conduct prisoners to different points. Tommy is just as liable to be a prisoner as an escort.

"Estaminet." A French public house, or saloon, where muddy water is sold for beer.

F

Fag. Cigarette. Something Tommy is always touching you for.

"Fag issue." Army issue of cigarettes, generally on Sunday.

Fatigue. Various kinds of work done by Tommy while he is "resting."

"Fed up." Disgusted; got enough of it—as the rich Mr. Hoggenheimer used to say, "Sufficiency."

Field Dressing. Bandages issued to soldiers for first aid when wounded. They use them for handkerchiefs and to clean their rifles.

Field Post Card. A card on which Tommy is allowed to tell his family and friends that he is alive; if he is dead the War Office sends a card, sometimes.

Field Punishment No. 1. Official name for spread-eagling a man on a limber wheel, two hours a day for twenty-one days. His rations consist of bully beef, water, and biscuits. Tommy calls this punishment "Crucifixion," especially if he has undergone it.

"Fifteen-pounder." Still another of ours; shell weighs fifteen pounds. Used for killing rats on the German parapets.

"Finding the range." Ascertaining by instrument or by trial shots the distance from an enemy objective.

"Fireworks." A night bombardment.

Fire Sector. A certain space of ground which a machine gun is supposed to sweep with its fire. If the gun refuses to work, all of the enemy who cross this space are technically dead, according to the General's plans.

Firing Squad. Twelve men picked to shoot a soldier who has been sentenced to death by court-martial. Tommy has no comment to make on this.

Firing Step. A ledge in the front trench which enables Tommy to fire "over the top." In rainy weather you have to be an acrobat to even stand on it on account of the slippery mud.

Fire Trench. The front-line trench. Another name for Hell.

"Five rounds rapid." Generally, just before daylight in the trenches, the order "Five rounds rapid" is given. Each man puts his rifle and head over the parapet and fires five shots as rapidly as possible in the direction of the German trenches and then ducks. A sort of "Good morning, have you used Pears Soap?"

"Five nine." A German shell 5.9 inches in diameter. It is their standard shell. Tommy has no special love for this brand, but they are like olives, all right when you get used to them.

"Flags." Tommy's nickname for a Signaler.

Flare. A rocket fired from a pistol which, at night, lights up the ground in front of your trench.

Flare Pistol. A large pistol, which looks like a sawed-off shotgun, from which flares are fired. When you need this pistol badly it has generally been left in your dugout.

Flying Column. A flying column of troops that *walk* from one point of the line to another. In case of need they usually arrive at the wrong point.

Fokker. A type of German aëroplane which the Boche claims to be the fastest in the world. Tommy believes this, because our airmen seldom catch them.

"For it." On the crime sheet; up against a reprimand; on trial, in trouble.

"Four by two." A piece of flannel four inches by two issued by the Q. M. Sergeant with which to "pull through."

"Four point five." Another of ours. The Germans don't like this one.

"Four point seven." One of our shells 4.7 inches in diameter. Tommy likes this kind.

"Fritz." Tommy's name for a German. He loves a German like poison.

Front Line. The nearest trench to the enemy. No place for a conscientious objector.

Frostbite. A quick road to Blighty, which Tommy used very often until frostbite became a court-martial offence. Now he keeps his feet warm.

"Full pack." A soldier carrying all of his equipment.

Full Corporal. A N. C. O. who sports two stripes on his arm and has more to say than the Colonel.

Fumigator. An infernal device at a hospital which cooks Tommy's uniform and returns it to him two sizes too small.

"Funk Hole." Tommy's term for a dugout. A favorite spot for those of a nervous disposition.

Fuse. A part of shell or bomb which burns in a set time and ignites the detonator.

G

Gas. Poisonous fumes which the Germans send over to our trenches. When the wind is favorable this gas is discharged into the air from huge cylinders. The wind carries it over toward our lines. It appears like a huge yellowish-green cloud rolling along the ground. The alarm is sounded and Tommy promptly puts on his gas helmet and laughs at the Boches.

Gas Gong. An empty shell case hung up in the trenches and in billets. A sentry is posted near it, so that in case German poison gas comes over, he can give the alarm by striking this gong with an iron bar. If the sentry happens to be asleep we get "gassed."

" Gassed." A soldier who has been overcome from the fumes of German poison gas, or the hot air of a comrade.

" Gassing." A term Tommy applies to "shooting the bull."

" Getting a sub." Touching an officer for money. To be taken out of soldier's pay on the next pay-day.

" Getting the sparks." Bullets from a machine gun cutting enemy barbed wire at night; when a bullet strikes wire it generally throws off a bluish spark. Machine gunners use this method at night to "set" their gun so that its fire will command the enemy's trench.

" Ginger." Nickname of a red-headed soldier; courage; pep.

" Gippo." Bacon grease; soup.

G. M. P. Garrison Military Police. Soldiers detailed to patrol the roads and regulate traffic behind the lines. Tommy's pet aversion.

G. O. C. General Officer Commanding. Tommy never sees him in the act of "commanding," but has the opportunity of reading many an order signed "G. O. C."

Goggles. An apparatus made of canvas and mica which is worn over the eyes for protection from the gases of German "tear shells." The only time Tommy cries is when he forgets his goggles or misses the rum issue.

" Going in." Taking over trenches.

" Going out." Relieved from the trenches.

" Gone West." Killed; died.

" Gooseberries." A wooden frame in the shape of a cask wrapped round with barbed wire. These gooseberries are thrown into the barbed-wire entanglements to help make them impassable.

" Got the Crown." Promoted to Sergeant-Major.

Green Envelope. An envelope of a green color issued to Tommy once a week. The contents will not be censored regiment-ally, but are liable to censor at the base. On the outside of envelope appears the following certificate, which Tommy must sign: "I certify on my honor that the contents of this envelope refer to nothing but private and family matters." After signing this certificate Tommy immediately writes about everything but family and private matters.

Groom. A soldier who looks after an officer's horse and who robs said horse of its hay. He makes his own bed comfortable with this hay.

Grousing. A scientific grumbling in which Tommy cusses everything in general and offends no one.

G. S. W. Gunshot wound. When Tommy is wounded he does not care whether it is a G. S. W. or a kick from a mule, just so he gets back to Blighty.

G. S. Wagon. A four-wheeled wagon driven by an A. S. C. driver. It carries supplies, such as food, ammunition, trench tools, and timber for dugouts. When Tommy gets sore feet he is allowed to ride on this wagon and fills the ears of the driver with tales of his wonderful exploits. Occasionally one of these drivers believes him.

Gum Boots. Rubber boots issued to Tommy for wet trenches. They are used to keep his feet dry; they do, when he is lucky enough to get a pair.

"Gumming the game." Spoiling anything, interfering.

H

"Hair brush." Name of a bomb used in the earlier stages of the war. It is shaped like a hair brush and is thrown by the handle. Tommy used to throw them over to the Germans for their morning toilette.

"Hand grenade." A general term for a bomb which is thrown by hand. Tommy looks upon all bombs with grave suspicion; from long experience he has learned not to trust them, even if the detonator has been removed.

"Hard tails." Mules.

Haversack. A canvas bag forming part of Tommy's equipment, carried on the left side. Its original use was intended for the carrying of emergency rations and small kit. It is generally filled with a miscellaneous assortment of tobacco, pipes, bread crumbs, letters, and a lot of useless souvenirs.

"Having a doss." Having a sleep.

"Hold-all." A small canvas roll in which you are supposed to carry your razor, comb, knife, fork, spoon, mirror, soap, tooth brush, etc. Tommy takes great care of the above, because it means extra pack drill to come on parade unshaven.

"Holy Joe." Tommy's familiar but not necessarily irreverent name for the Chaplain. He really has a great admiration for this officer, who although not a fighting man, so often risks his life to save a wounded Tommy.

"Housewife." A neat little package of needles, thread, extra shoelaces, and buttons. When a button comes off Tommy's trousers, instead of going to his housewife he looks around for a nail.

Hun. Another term for a German, mostly used by war correspondents.

"Hun pinching." Raiding German trenches for prisoners.

I

Identification Disk. A little fiber disk which is worn around the neck by means of a string. On one side is stamped your name, rank, regimental number, and regiment, while on the other side is stamped your religion. If at any time Tommy is doubtful of his identity he looks at his disk to reassure himself.

"I'm sorry." Tommy's apology. If he pokes your eye out with his bayonet he says, "I'm sorry," and the matter is ended so far as he is concerned.

"In front." Over the top; in front of the front-line trench, in No Man's Land.

"In reserve." Troops occupying positions, billets, or dugouts, immediately in rear of the front line, who in case of an attack will support the firing line.

Intelligence Department. Secret service men who are supposed to catch spies or be spies as the occasion demands.

Interpreter. A fat job with a "return ticket," held by a soldier who thinks he can speak a couple of languages. He questions prisoners as to the color of their grandmothers' eyes and why they joined the army. Just imagine asking a German "why" he joined the army.

"Invalided." Sent to England on account of sickness.

Iron Rations. A tin of bully beef, two biscuits, and a tin containing tea, sugar, and Oxo cubes. These are not supposed to be eaten until you die of starvation.

Isolated Post. An advanced part of a trench or position where one or two sentries are posted to guard against a surprise attack. While in this post Tommy is constantly wondering what the Germans will do with his body.

" It's good we have a Navy." One of Tommy's expressions when he is disgusted with the army and its work.

J

" Jack Johnson." A seventeen-inch German shell. Probably called "Jack Johnson" because the Germans thought that with it they could lick the world.

Jackknife. A knife, issued to Tommy, which weighs a stone and won't cut. Its only virtue is the fact that it has a tin-opener attachment which won't open tins.

Jam. A horrible mess of fruit and sugar which Tommy spreads on his bread. It all tastes the same no matter whether labelled "Strawberry" or "Green Gage."

" Jam Tin." A crude sort of hand grenade which, in the early stages of the war, Tommy used to manufacture out of jam tins, ammonal, and mud. The manufacturer generally would receive a little wooden cross in recognition of the fact that he died for King and Country.

Jock. Universal name for a Scotchman.

K

" Kicked the bucket." Died.

Kilo. Five eighths of a mile. Ten "kilos" generally means a trek of fifteen miles.

" King's Shilling." Tommy's rate of pay per day, perhaps. "Taking the King's Shilling" means enlisting.

" Kip." Tommy's term for "sleep." He also calls his bed his "kip." It is on guard that Tommy most desires to kip.

Kit Bag. A part of Tommy's equipment in which he is supposed to pack up his troubles and smile, according to the words of a popular song (the composer was never in a trench).

Kitchener's Army. The volunteer army raised by Lord Kitchener, the members of which signed for duration of war. They are commonly called the "New Army" or "Kitchener's Mob." At first the Regulars and Territorials looked down on them, but now accept them as welcome mates.

L

Labor Battalion. An organization which is "too proud to fight." They would sooner use a pick and shovel.

Lance-Corporal. A N. C. O. one grade above a private who wears a shoestring stripe on his arm and thinks the war should be run according to his ideas.

" Lead. " The leading pair of horses or mules on a limber. Their only fault is that they won't lead (if they happen to be mules).

Leave Train. The train which takes Tommy to one of the seaports on the Channel *en route* to Blighty when granted leave. The worst part of going on leave is coming back.

Lee Enfield. Name of the rifle used by the British Army. Its caliber is .303 and the magazine holds ten rounds. When dirty it has a nasty habit of getting Tommy's name on the crime sheet.

" Legging it. " Running away.

Lewis Gun. A rifle-like machine gun, air cooled, which only carries 47 rounds in its "pie-plate" magazine. Under fire when this magazine is emptied you shout for "ammo" but perhaps No. 2, the ammo carrier, is lying in the rear with a bullet through his napper. Then it's "napoo-fini" (Tommy's French) for Mr. Lewis.

" Light Duty." What the doctor marks on the sick report opposite a Tommy's name when he has doubts as to whether said Tommy is putting one over on him. Usually Tommy is.

Light Railway. Two thin iron tracks on which small flat cars full of ammunition and supplies are pushed. These railways afford Tommy great sport in the loading, pushing, and unloading of cars.

Limber. A match box on two wheels which gives the Army mule a job. It also carries officer's packs.

Liquid Fire. Another striking example of German "Kultur."

According to the Germans it is supposed to annihilate whole brigades, but Tommy refuses to be annihilated.

Listening Post. Two or three men detailed to go out "in front" at night, to lie on the ground and listen for any undue activity in the German lines. They also listen for the digging of mines. It is nervous work and when Tommy returns he generally writes for a box of "Phosperine Tablets," a widely advertised nerve tonic.

"Little Willie." Tommy's nickname for the German Crown Prince. They are not on speaking terms.

"Lloyd George's Pets." Munition workers in England.

"Lonely Soldier." A soldier who advertises himself as "lonely" through the medium of some English newspaper. If he is clever and diplomatic by this method he generally receives two or three parcels a week, but he must be careful not to write to two girls living on the same block or his parcel post mail will diminish.

"Lonely Stab." A girl who writes and sends parcels to Tommy. She got his name from the "Lonely Soldier Column" of some newspaper.

Loophole. A disguised aperture in a trench through which to "snipe" at Germans.

Lyddite. A high explosive used in shells. Has a habit of scattering bits of anatomy over the landscape.

M

M. G. C. Machine Gun Corps. A collection of machine gunners who think they are the deciding factor of the war, and that artillery is unnecessary.

M. G. Machine Gunner. A man who, like an American policeman, is never there when he is badly wanted.

Maconochie. A ration of meat, vegetables, and soapy water, contained in a tin. Mr. Maconochie, the chemist who compounded this mess, intends to commit "hari kari" before the boys return from the front. He is wise.

"Mad Minute." Firing fifteen rounds from your rifle in sixty seconds. A man is mad to attempt it, especially with a stiff bolt.

Mail Bag. A canvas bag which is used to bring the other fellow's mail around.

Major. An officer in a Battalion who wears a crown on his uniform, is in command of two companies, and corrects said companies in the second position of "present arms." He also resides in a dugout.

Maneuvers. Useless evolutions of troops conceived by someone higher up to show Tommy how brave his officers are and how battles *should* be fought. The enemy never attend these maneuvers to prove they're right.

Mass Formation. A close order formation in which the Germans attack. It gives them a sort of "Come on, I'm with you" feeling. They would "hold hands" only for the fact that they have to carry their rifles. Tommy takes great delight in "busting up" these gatherings.

Mate. A soldier with whom Tommy is especially "chummy." Generally picked because this soldier receives a parcel from home every week.

Maxim. Type of machine gun which has been supplanted by the Vickers in order to make Tommy unlearn what he has been taught about the Maxim.

M. T. Mechanical Transport. The members of which are ex-taxi drivers. No wonder Tommy's rations melt away when the M. T. carries them.

M. O. Medical Officer. A doctor specially detailed to tell Tommy that he is not sick.

"M. and D." What the doctor marks on the "sicker" or sick report when he thinks Tommy is faking sickness. It means medicine and duty.

Mentioned in Despatches. Recommended for bravery. Tommy would sooner be recommended for leave.

"Mercy Kamerad." What Fritz says when he has had a bellyful of fighting and wants to surrender. Of late this has been quite a popular phrase with him, replacing the Hymn of Hate.

Mess Orderly. A soldier detailed daily to carry Tommy's meals to and from the cook-house.

Mess Tin. An article of equipment used as a tea-kettle and dinner-set.

"Mike and George." K. C. M. G. (Knight Commander of the Order of St. Michael and St. George). An award for bravery in the field.

Military Cross. A badge of honor dished out to officers for bravery. Tommy insists they throw dice to see which is the bravest. The winner gets the medal.

Military Medal. A piece of junk issued to Tommy who has done something that is not exactly brave but still is not cowardly. When it is presented he takes it and goes back wondering why the Army picks on him.

M. P. Military Police. Soldiers with whom it is unsafe to argue.

" Mills. " Name of a bomb invented by Mills. The only bomb in which Tommy has full confidence,—and he mistrusts even that.

Mine. An underground tunnel dug by sappers of the Royal Engineer Corps. This tunnel leads from your trench to that of the enemy's. At the end or head of the tunnel a great quantity of explosives are stored which at a given time are exploded. It is Tommy's job to then go "over the top" and occupy the crater caused by the explosion.

Mine Shaft. A shaft leading down to the "gallery" or tunnel of a mine. Sometimes Tommy, as a reward, is given the job of helping the R. E.'s dig this shaft.

Minnenwerfer. A high-power trench mortar shell of the Germans, which makes no noise coming through the air. It was invented by Professor Kultur. Tommy does not know it is near until it bites him; after that nothing worries him. Tommy nicknames them "Minnies."

Mouth Organ. An instrument with which a vindictive Tommy causes misery to the rest of his platoon. Some authorities define it as a "musical instrument."

Mud. A brownish, sticky substance found in the trenches after the frequent rains. A true friend to Tommy, which sticks to him like glue, even though at times Tommy resents this affection and roundly curses said mud.

Mufti. The term Tommy gives to civilian clothes. Mufti looks good to him now.

N

Nap. A card game of Tommy's in which the one who stays awake the longest grabs the pot. If all the players fall asleep, the pot goes to the "Wounded Soldiers' Fund."

"Napoo-Fini." Tommy's French for gone, through with, finished, disappeared.

"Napper." Tommy's term for head.

Neutral. Tommy says it means "afraid to fight."

Next of Kin. Nearest relative. A young and ambitious platoon officer bothers his men two or three times a month taking a record of their "next of kin," because he thinks that Tommy's grandmother may have changed to his uncle.

"Night ops." Slang for night operations or maneuvers.

Nine-point-two. A howitzer which fires a shell 9.2 inches in diameter, and knocks the tiles off the roof of Tommy's billet through the force of its concussion.

No Man's Land. The space between the hostile trenches called "No Man's Land" because no one owns it and no one wants to. In France you could not give it away.

N. C. C. Non-Combatant Corps. Men who joined the Army under the stipulation that the only thing they would fight for would be their meals. They have no "King and Country."

N. C. O. Non-commissioned officer. A person hated more than the Germans. Tommy says his stripes are issued out with the rations, and he ought to know.

"No. 9." A pill the doctor gives you if you are suffering with corns or barber's itch or any disease at all. If none are in stock, he gives you a No. 6 and No. 3, or a No. 5 and No. 4, anything to make nine.

Nosecap. That part of a shell which unscrews and contains the device and scale for setting the time fuse. Some Tommies are ardent souvenir hunters. As soon as a shell bursts in the ground you will see them out with picks and shovels digging in the shell hole for the nose cap. If the shell bursts too near them they don't dig.

O

Observation Balloon. A captive balloon behind the lines which observes the enemy. The enemy doesn't mind being observed, so takes no notice of it. It gives someone a job hauling it down at night, so it has one good point.

Observation Post. A position in the front line where an artillery officer observes the fire of our guns. He keeps on observing until a German shell observes him. After this there is generally a new officer and a new observation post.

O. C. Officer commanding.

Officers' Mess. Where the officers eat the mess that the O. S. have cooked.

O. S. Officers' servants. The lowest ranking private in the Army, who feeds better than the officers he waits on.

"Oil Cans." Tommy's term for a German trench mortar shell, which is an old tin filled with explosive and junk that the Boches have no further use for.

"One up." Tommy's term for a lance-corporal who wears one stripe. The private always wonders why he was overlooked when promotions were in order.

"On the mat." When Tommy is haled before his commanding officer to explain why he has broken one of the seven million King's regulations for the government of the Army. His "explanation" never gets him anywhere unless it is on the wheel of a limber.

"On your own." Another famous or infamous phrase which means Tommy is allowed to do as he pleases. An officer generally puts Tommy "on his own" when he gets Tommy into a dangerous position and sees no way to extricate him.

Orderly-Corporal. A non-commissioned officer who takes the names of the sick every morning and who keeps his own candle burning after he has ordered "Lights out" at night.

Orderly-Officer. An officer who, for a week, goes around and asks if there are "any complaints" and gives the name of the complaining soldier to the Orderly-Sergeant for extra pack drill.

Orderly Room. The Captain's office where everything is disorderly.

Orderly-Sergeant. A sergeant who, for a week, is supposed to do the work of the Orderly-Officer.

"Out of bounds." The official Army term meaning that Tommy is not allowed to trespass where this sign is displayed. He never wished to until the sign made its appearance.

"Out there." A term used in Blighty which means "in France." Conscientious objectors object to going "out there."

" Over the Top. " A famous phrase of the trenches. It is
generally the order for the men to charge the German lines.
Nearly always it is accompanied by the Jonah wish, "With
the best o' luck and give them hell."

Oxo. Concentrated beef cubes that a fond mother sends out to
Tommy because they are advertised as "British to the
Backbone."

P

Packing. Asbestos wrapping around the barrel of a machine
gun to keep the water from leaking out of the barrel casing.
Also slang for rations.

Pack Drill. Punishment for a misdemeanor. Sometimes Tommy
gets caught when he fills his pack with straw to lighten it
for this drill.

Parados. The rear wall of a trench which the Germans continu-
ally fill with bits of shell and rifle bullets. Tommy doesn't
mind how many they put in the parados.

Parapet. The top part of a front trench which Tommy constantly builds up and the Germans just as constantly knock
down.

Patrol. A few soldiers detailed to go out in "No Man's Land,"
at night and return without any information. Usually these
patrols are successful.

Pay Book. A little book in which is entered the amount of pay
Tommy draws. In the back of same there is also a space for
his "will and last testament"; this to remind Tommy that
he is liable to be killed. (As if he needed any reminder.)

Pay Parade. A formation at which Tommy lines up for pay.
When his turn comes the paying-officer asks, "How much?"
and Tommy answers, "Fifteen francs, sir." He gets five.

Periscope. A thing in the trenches which you look through.
After looking through it, you look over the top to really see
something.

" Physical torture." The nickname for physical training. It is
torture, especially to a recruit.

Pick. A tool shaped like an anchor which is being constantly
handed to Tommy with the terse command, "get busy."

Pioneer. A soldier detailed in each company to keep the space around the billets clean. He sleeps all day and only gets busy when an officer comes round. He also sleeps at night.

" Pip squeak. " Tommy's term for a small German shell which makes a "pip" and then a "squeak," when it comes over.

Poilu. French term, for their private soldier. Tommy would use it and sometimes does, but each time he pronounces it differently, so no one knows what he is talking about.

Pontoon. A card game, in America known as "Black Jack" or "Twenty One." The banker is the only winner.

Provost-Sergeant. A sergeant detailed to oversee prisoners, their work, etc. Each prisoner solemnly swears that when he gets out of "clink" he is going to shoot this sergeant and when he does get out he buys him a drink.

Pull Through. A stout cord with a weight on one end, and a loop on the other for an oily rag. The weighted end is dropped through the bore of the rifle and the rag on the other end is "pulled through."

Pump. A useless contrivance for emptying the trenches of water. "Useless" because the trenches refuse to be emptied.

" Pushing up the Daisies. " Tommy's term for a soldier who has been killed and buried in France.

Q

" Queer." Tommy's term for being sick. The doctor immediately informs him that there is nothing queer about him, and Tommy doesn't know whether to feel insulted or complimented.

Quid. Tommy's term for a pound or twenty shillings (about $4.80). He is not on very good terms with this amount as you never see the two together.

Q. M.-Sergeant. Quartermaster-Sergeant, or "Quarter" as he is called. A non-commissioned officer in a company who wears three stripes and a crown, and takes charge of the company stores, with the emphasis on the "takes." In civil life he was a politician or burglar.

R

Range Finder. An instrument for ascertaining the distance between two objects, using the instrument as one object.

It is very accurate only you get a different result each time you use it, says Tommy.

Rapid Fire. Means to stick your head "over the top" at night, aim at the moon, and empty your magazine. If there is no moon, aim at the spot where it should be.

Ration Bag. A small, very small bag for carrying rations. Sometimes it is really useful for lugging souvenirs.

Rations. Various kinds of tasteless food issued by the Government to Tommy, to kid him into thinking that he is living in luxury, while the Germans are starving.

Ration Party. Men detailed to carry rations to the front line; pick out a black, cold, and rainy night; put a fifty-pound box on your shoulder; sling your rifle and carry one hundred twenty rounds of ammunition. Then go through a communication trench, with the mud up to your knees, down this trench for a half-mile, and then find your mates swearing in seven different languages; duck a few shells and bullets, and then ask Tommy for his definition of a "ration party." You will be surprised to learn that it is the same as yours.

Rats. The main inhabitants of the trenches and dugouts. Very useful for chewing up leather equipment and running over your face when asleep. A British rat resembles a bulldog, while a German one, through a course of Kultur, resembles a dachshund.

"Red Cap." Tommy's nickname for a Staff Officer because he wears a red band around his cap.

Red Tape. A useless sort of procedure. The main object of this is to prolong the war and give a lot of fat jobs to Army politicians.

Regimental Number. Each soldier has a number whether or not he was a convict in civil life. Tommy never forgets his number when he sees it on "orders for leave."

R. P. Regimental Police. Men detailed in a Battalion to annoy Tommy and to prevent him from doing what he most desires.

Reinforcements. A lot of new men sent out from England who think that the war will be over a week after they enter the trenches.

Relaying. A term used by the artillery. After a gun is fired it is "relayed" or aimed at something out of sight.

20

Respirator. A cloth helmet, chemically treated, with glass eye-holes, which Tommy puts over his head as a protection against poison gas. This helmet never leaves Tommy's person, he even sleeps with it.

Rest. A period of time for rest allotted to Tommy upon being relieved from the trenches. He uses this "rest" to mend roads, dig trenches, and make himself generally useful while behind the lines.

Rest Billets. Shell shattered houses, generally barns, in which Tommy "rests," when relieved from the firing line.

" Ricco. " Term for a ricochet bullet. It makes a whining noise and Tommy always ducks when a "ricco" passes him.

Rifle. A part of Tommy's armament. Its main use is to be cleaned. Sometimes it is fired, when you are not using a pick or shovel. You also "present arms by numbers" with it. This is a very fascinating exercise to Tommy. Ask him.

Rifle Grenade. A bomb on the end of a rod. This rod is inserted into the barrel of a specially designed rifle.

" R. I. P. " In monk's highbrow, "Requiscat in pace," put on little wooden crosses over soldier's graves. It means "Rest in peace," but Tommy says like as not it means "Rest in pieces," especially if the man under the cross has been sent West by a bomb or shell explosion.

" Road Dangerous, Use Trench. " A familiar sign on roads immediately in rear of the firing line. It is to warn soldiers that it is within sight of Fritz. Tommy never believes these signs and swanks up the road. Later on he tells the Red Cross nurse that the sign told the truth.

" Roll of Honor. " The name given to the published casualty lists of the war. Tommy has no ambition for his name to appear on the "Roll of Honor" unless it comes under the heading "Slightly Wounded."

R. C. Roman Catholic. One of the advantages of being a R. C., is that "Church Parade" is not compulsory.

" Rooty. " Tommy's nickname for bread.

Route March. A useless expenditure of leather and energy. These marches teach Tommy to be kind to overloaded beasts of burden.

R. A. M. C. Royal Army Medical Corps. Tommy says it means "Rob All My Comrades."

R. E.'s. Royal Engineers.

R. F. A.'s. Royal Field Artillery men.

R. F. C.'s. Royal Flying Corps.

Rum. A nectar of the gods issued in the early morning to Tommy.

Rum issue. A daily formation at which Tommy receives a spoonful of rum; that is if any is left over from the Sergeant's Mess.

Runner. A soldier who is detailed or picked as an orderly for an officer while in the trenches. His real job is to take messages under fire, asking how many tins of jam are required for 1917.

S

S. A. A. Small Arms Ammunition. Small steel pellets which have a bad habit of drilling holes in the anatomy of Tommy and Fritz.

Salvo. Battery firing four guns simultaneously.

Sandbag. A jute bag which is constantly being filled with earth. Its main uses are to provide Tommy with material for a comfortable kip and to strengthen parapets.

Sap. A small ditch, or trench, dug from the front line and leading out into "No Man's Land" in the direction of the German trenches.

Sapper. A man who saps or digs mines. He thinks he is thirty-three degrees above an ordinary soldier, while in fact he is generally beneath him.

Sausage Balloon. See observation balloon.

S. B. Stretcher Bearer. The motive power of a stretcher. He is generally looking the other way when a fourteen-stone Tommy gets hit.

Scaling ladder. Small wooden ladders used by Tommy for climbing out of the front trench when he goes "over the top." When Tommy sees these ladders being brought into the trench, he sits down and writes his will in his little pay-book.

Sentry Go. Time on guard. It means "sentry come."

Sergeant's Mess. Where the sergeants eat. Nearly all of the rum has a habit of disappearing into the Sergeant's Mess.

Seventy-fives. A very efficient field-gun of the French, which can fire thirty shells per minute. The gun needs no relaying due to the recoil which throws the gun back to its original position. The gun that knocked out "Jack Johnson," therefore called "Jess Willard."

" Sewed in a blanket. " Term for a soldier who has been buried. His remains are generally sewn in a blanket and the piece of blanket is generally deducted from his pay that is due.

Shag. Cigarette tobacco which an American can never learn to use. Even the mules object to the smell of it.

Shell. A device of the artillery which sometimes makes Tommy wish he had been born in a neutral country.

Shell Hole. A hole in the ground caused by the explosion of a shell. Tommy's favorite resting-place while under fire.

Shovel. A tool closely related to the pick family. In France the "shovel" is mightier than the sword.

Shrapnel. A shell which bursts in the air and scatters small pieces of metal over a large area. It is used to test the resisting power of steel helmets.

" Sicker. " Nickname for the sick report book. It is Tommy's ambition to get on this "sicker" without feeling sick.

Sick Parade. A formation at which the doctor informs sick, or would-be sick Tommies that they are not sick.

Sixty-pounder. One of our shells which weighs sixty pounds (officially). When Tommy handles them, their *unofficial* weight is three hundred weight.

Slacker. An insect in England who is afraid to join the Army. There are three things in this world that Tommy hates: a slacker, a German, and a trench-rat; it's hard to tell which he hates worst.

" Slag Heap." A pile of rubbish, tin cans, etc.

Smoke Bomb. A shell which, in exploding, emits a dense white smoke, hiding the operations of troops. When Tommy, in attacking a trench, gets into this smoke, he imagines himself a magnet and thinks all the machine guns and rifles are firing at him alone.

Smoke Helmet. See respirator.

Sniper. A good shot whose main occupation is picking off unwary individuals of the enemy. In the long run a sniper usually gets "sniped."

Snipe Hole. A hole in a steel plate through which snipers "snipe." It is not fair for the enemy to shoot at these holes, but they do, and often hit them, or at least the man behind them.

" Soldiers' Friend." Metal polish costing three ha' pence which Tommy uses to polish his buttons. Tommy wonders why it is called "Soldiers' Friend."

" Somewhere in France. " A certain spot in France where Tommy has to live in mud, hunt for "cooties," and duck shells and bullets. Tommy's official address.

Souvenir. A begging word used by the French kiddies. When it is addressed to Tommy it generally means, a penny, biscuits, bully beef, or a tin of jam.

Spy. A suspicious person whom no one suspects until he is caught. Then all say they knew he was a spy but had no chance to report it to the proper authorities.

" Spud. " Tommy's name for the solitary potato which gets into the stew. It's a great mystery how that lonely little spud got into such bad company.

Stand To. Order to mount the fire step. Given just as it begins to grow dark.

Stand Down. Order given in the trenches at break of dawn to let the men know their night watch is ended. It has a pleasant sound in Tommy's ears.

Star Shell. See Flare.

Steel Helmet. A round hat made out of steel which is supposed to be shrapnel proof. It is until a piece of shell goes through it, then Tommy loses interest as to whether it is shrapnel proof or not. He calls it a "tin hat."

Stew. A concoction of the cook's which contains bully beef, Maconochie rations, water, a few lumps of fresh meat, and a potato. Occasionally a little salt falls into it by mistake. Tommy is supposed to eat this mess—he does—worse luck!

" Strafeing. " Tommy's chief sport—shelling the Germans. Taken from Fritz's own dictionary.

Stretcher. A contrivance on which dead and wounded are carried. The only time Tommy gets a free ride in the trenches is while on a stretcher. As a rule he does not appreciate this means of transportation.

" Suicide Club." Nickname for bombers and machine gunners. (No misnomer.)

Supper. Tommy's fourth meal, generally eaten just before "lights out." It is composed of the remains of the day's rations. There are a lot of Tommies who never eat supper There is a reason.

S. W. Shell wound. What the doctor marks on your hospita chart when a shell has removed your leg.

Swamping. Putting on airs; showing off. Generally accredited to Yankees.

" Swinging the lead." Throwing the bull.

" Sweating on leave." Impatiently waiting for your name to appear in orders for leave. If Tommy sweats very long he generally catches cold and when leave comes he is too sick to go.

T

" Taking over." Going into a trench. Tommy " takes over," is " taken out," and sometimes is " put under."

Taube. A type of German aëroplane whose special ambition is beating the altitude record. It occasionally loses its way and flies over the British lines and then stops flying.

Tea. A dark brown drug, which Tommy has to have at certain periods of the day. Battles have been known to have been stopped to enable Tommy to get his tea, or "char" as it is commonly called.

"Tear Shell." Trench name for the German lachrymose chemical shell which makes the eyes smart. The only time Tommy is outwardly sentimental.

Telephone. A little instrument with a wire attached to it. An artillery observer whispers something into this instrument and immediately one of your batteries behind the line opens up and drops a few shells into your front trench. This keeps up until the observer whispers, "Your range is too short." Then the shells drop nearer the German lines.

"**Terrier.**" Tommy's nickname for a Territorial or "Saturday-night soldier." A regular despises a Territorial while a Territorial looks down on "Kitchener's Mob." Kitchener's Mob has the utmost contempt for both of them.

Territorial. A peace-time soldier with the same status as the American militiaman. Before the war they were called "Saturday-Night Soldiers," but they soon proved themselves "every-night soldiers."

"**The Old Man.**" Captain of a company. He is called "the old man," because generally his age is about twenty-eight.

"**The Best o' Luck.**" The Jonah phrase of the trenches. Every time Tommy goes over the top or on a trench raid his mates wish him the best o' luck. It means that if you are lucky enough to come back, you generally have an arm or leg missing.

"**Thumbs up.**" Tommy's expression which means "everything is fine with me." Very seldom used during an intense bombardment.

"**Time ex.**" Expiration of term of enlistment. The only time Tommy is a civilian in the trenches; but about ten minutes after he is a soldier for duration of war.

"**Tin Hat.**" Tommy's name for his steel helmet which is made out of a metal about as hard as mush. The only advantage is that it is heavy and greatly adds to the weight of Tommy's equipment. Its most popular use is for carrying eggs.

T. N. T. A high explosive which the Army Ordnance Corps prescribes for Fritz. Fritz prefers a No. 9 pill.

"**Tommy Atkins.**" The name England gives to an English soldier, even if his name is Willie Jones.

Tommy's Cooker. A spirit stove widely advertised as "A suitable gift to the men in the trenches." Many are sent out to Tommy and most of them are thrown away.

Tonite. The explosive contained in a rifle grenade. It looks like a harmless reel of cotton before it explodes,—after it explodes the spectator is missing.

"**Toots Sweet.**" Tommy's French for "hurry up," "look smart." Generally used in a French *estaminet* when Tommy only has a couple of minutes in which to drink his beer.

" Top Hats at Home. " Tommy's name for Parliament when his application for leave has been turned down or when no strawberry jam arrives with the rations.

Town Major. An officer stationed in a French town or village who is supposed to look after billets, upkeep of roads, and act as interpreter.

Transport. An aggregation of mules, limbers, and rough riders, whose duty is to keep the men in the trenches supplied with rations and supplies. Sometimes a shell drops within two miles of them and Tommy doesn't get his rations, etc.

Traverse. Sandbags piled in a trench so that the trench cannot be traversed by Tommy. Sometimes it prevents enfilading fire by the enemy.

Trench. A ditch full of water, rats, and soldiers. During his visit to France, Tommy uses these ditches as residences. Now and again he sticks his head "over the top" to take a look at the surrounding scenery. If he is lucky he lives to tell his mates what he saw.

Trench Feet. A disease of the feet contracted in the trenches from exposure to extreme cold and wet. Tommy's greatest ambition is to contract this disease because it means "Blighty" for him.

Trench Fever. A malady contracted in the trenches; the symptoms are high temperature, bodily pains, and homesickness. Mostly homesickness. A bad case lands Tommy in "Blighty," a slight case lands him back in the trenches, where he tries to get it worse than ever.

" Trenchitis. " A combination of "fedupness" and homesickness, experienced by Tommy in the trenches, especially when he receives a letter from a friend in Blighty who is making a fortune working in a munition plant.

Trench Mortar. A gun like a stove pipe which throws shells at the German trenches. Tommy detests these mortars because when they take positions near to him in the trenches, he knows that it is only a matter of minutes before a German shell with his name and number on it will be knocking at his door.

Trench Pudding. A delectable mess of broken biscuits, condensed milk, jam, and mud, slightly flavored with smoke.

Tommy prepares, cooks, and eats this. Next day he has "trench fever."

Trench Raid. Several men detailed to go over the top at night and shake hands with the Germans, and, if possible, persuade some of them to be prisoners. At times the raiders would themselves get raided because Fritz refused to shake and adopted nasty methods.

Turpenite. A deadly chemical shell invented by an enthusiastic war correspondent suffering from brain storm. Companies and batteries were supposed to die standing up from its effects, but they refused to do this.

" Twelve in one. " Means that twelve men are to share one loaf of bread. When the slicing takes place the war in the dug-out makes the European argument look like thirty cents.

U

" Up against the wall. " Tommy's term for a man who is to be shot by a firing squad.

" Up the line. " Term generally used in rest billets when Tommy talks about the fire trench or fighting line. When orders are issued to go "up the line" Tommy immediately goes "up in the air."

V

V. C. Victoria Cross, or "Very careless" as Tommy calls it. It is a bronze medal won by Tommy for being very careless with his life.

Very-Lights. A star shell invented by Mr. Very. See Flare.

Vickers Gun. A machine gun improved on by a fellow named Vickers. His intentions were good but his improvements, according to Tommy, were "rotten."

Vin Blanc. French white wine made from vinegar. They forgot the red ink.

Vin Rouge. French red wine made from vinegar and red ink. Tommy pays good money for it.

W

Waders. Rubber hip boots, used when the water in the trenches is up to Tommy's neck.

Waiting Man. The cleanest man at guard mounting. He does not have to walk post; is supposed to wait on the guard.

Washout. Tommy's idea of something that is worth nothing.

Water Bottle. A metal bottle for carrying water (when not used for rum, beer, or wine).

Waterproof. A rubber sheet issued to Tommy to keep him dry. It does when the sun is out.

Wave. A line of troops which goes "over the top" in a charge. The waves are numbered according to their turn in going over, viz., "First Wave," "Second Wave," etc. Tommy would sooner go over with the "Tenth Wave."

Wet Canteen. A military saloon or pub where Tommy can get a "wet." Most campaigns and battles are planned and fought in these places.

"Whizz Bang." A small German shell which whizzes through the air and explodes with a "bang." Their bark is worse than their bite.

"Wind up." Term generally applied to the Germans when they send up several star shells at once because they are nervous and expect an attack or night raid on their trenches.

"Windy." Tommy's name for a nervous soldier, coward.

"Wipers." Tommy's name for Ypres, sometimes he calls it "Yeeps." A place up the line which Tommy likes to duck. It is even "hot" in the winter time at "Wipers."

Wire. See barbed wire, but don't go "over the top" to look at it. It isn't safe.

Wire Cutters. An instrument for cutting barbed wire, but mostly used for driving nails.

Wiring Party. Another social affair for which Tommy receives invitations. It consists of going "over the top" at night and stretching barbed wire between stakes. A German machine gun generally takes the place of an orchestra.

Woodbine. A cigarette made of paper and old hay. Tommy swears by a Woodbine.

Wooden Cross. Two pieces of wood in the form of a cross placed at the head of a Tommy's grave. Inscribed on it are his rank, name, number, and regiment. Also date of death and last but not least, the letters R. I. P.

Working Party. A sort of compulsory invitation affair for which

Tommy often is honored with an invitation. It consists of digging, filling sandbags, and ducking shells and bullets.

Z

Zeppelin. A bag full of gas invented by a count full of gas. It is a dirigible airship used by the Germans for killing babies and dropping bombs in open fields. You never see them over the trenches, it is safer to bombard civilians in cities. They use Iron Crosses for ballast.

Popular Copyright Novels

AT MODERATE PRICES

Ask Your Dealer for a Complete List of
A. L. Burt Company's Popular Copyright Fiction

Abner Daniel. By Will N. Harben.
Adventures of Gerard. By A. Conan Doyle.
Adventures of a Modest Man. By Robert W. Chambers.
Adventures of Sherlock Holmes. By A. Conan Doyle.
Adventures of Jimmie Dale, The. By Frank L. Packard.
After House, The. By Mary Roberts Rinehart.
Alisa Paige. By Robert W. Chambers.
Alton of Somasco. By Harold Bindloss.
A Man's Man. By Ian Hay.
Amateur Gentleman, The. By Jeffery Farnol.
Andrew The Glad. By Maria Thompson Daviess.
Ann Boyd. By Will N. Harben.
Anna the Adventuress. By E. Phillips Oppenheim.
Another Man's Shoes. By Victor Bridges.
Ariadne of Allan Water. By Sidney McCall.
Armchair at the Inn, The. By F. Hopkinson Smith.
Around Old Chester. By Margaret Deland.
Athalie. By Robert W. Chambers.
At the Mercy of Tiberius. By Augusta Evans Wilson.
Auction Block, The. By Rex Beach.
Aunt Jane. By Jeanette Lee.
Aunt Jane of Kentucky. By Eliza C. Hall.
Awakening of Helena Richie. By Margaret Deland.

Bambi. By Marjorie Benton Cooke.
Bandbox, The. By Louis Joseph Vance.
Barbara of the Snows. By Harry Irving Green.
Bar 20. By Clarence E. Mulford.
Bar 20 Days. By Clarence E. Mulford.
Barrier, The. By Rex Beach.
Beasts of Tarzan, The. By Edgar Rice Burroughs.
Beechy. By Bettina Von Hutten.
Bella Donna. By Robert Hichens.
Beloved Vagabond, The. By Wm. J. Locke.
Beltane the Smith. By Jeffery Farnol.
Ben Blair. By Will Lillibridge.
Betrayal, The. By E. Phillips Oppenheim.
Better Man, The. By Cyrus Townsend Brady.
Beulah. (Ill. Ed.) By Augusta J. Evans.
Beyond the Frontier. By Randall Parrish.
Black Is White. By George Barr McCutcheon.

Popular Copyright Novels

AT MODERATE PRICES

Ask Your Dealer for a Complete List of
A. L. Burt Company's Popular Copyright Fiction

Blind Man's Eyes, The. By Wm. MacHarg & Edwin Balmer.
Bob Hampton of Placer. By Randall Parrish.
Bob, Son of Battle. By Alfred Ollivant.
Britton of the Seventh. By Cyrus Townsend Brady.
Broad Highway, The. By Jeffery Farnol.
Bronze Bell, The. By Louis Joseph Vance.
Bronze Eagle, The. By Baroness Orczy.
Buck Peters, Ranchman. By Clarence E. Mulford.
Business of Life, The. By Robert W. Chambers.
By Right of Purchase. By Harold Bindloss.

Cabbages and Kings. By O. Henry.
Calling of Dan Matthews, The. By Harold Bell Wright.
Cape Cod Stories. By Joseph C. Lincoln.
Cap'n Dan's Daughter. By Joseph C. Lincoln.
Cap'n Eri. By Joseph C. Lincoln.
Cap'n Warren's Wards. By Joseph C. Lincoln.
Cardigan. By Robert W. Chambers.
Carpet From Bagdad, The. By Harold MacGrath.
Cease Firing. By Mary Johnson.
Chain of Evidence, A. By Carolyn Wells.
Chief Legatee, The. By Anna Katharine Green.
Cleek of Scotland Yard. By T. W. Hanshew.
Clipped Wings. By Rupert Hughes.
Coast of Adventure, The. By Harold Bindloss.
Colonial Free Lance, A. By Chauncey C. Hotchkiss.
Coming of Cassidy, The By Clarence E. Mulford.
Coming of the Law, The. By Chas. A. Seltzer.
Conquest of Canaan, The. By Booth Tarkington.
Conspirators, The. By Robt. W. Chambers.
Counsel for the Defense. By Leroy Scott.
Court of Inquiry, A. By Grace S. Richmond.
Crime Doctor, The. By E. W. Hornung
Crimson Gardenia, The, and Other Tales of Adventure. By
    Rex Beach.
Cross Currents. By Eleanor H. Porter.
Cry in the Wilderness, A. By Mary E. Waller.
Cynthia of the Minute. By Louis Jos. Vance.

Dark Hollow, The. By Anna Katharine Green.
Dave's Daughter. By Patience Bevier Cole.

Popular Copyright Novels

AT MODERATE PRICES

Ask Your Dealer for a Complete List of
A. L. Burt Company's Popular Copyright Fiction

Day of Days, The. By Louis Joseph Vance.
Day of the Dog, The. By George Barr McCutcheon.
Depot Master, The. By Joseph C. Lincoln.
Desired Woman, The. By Will N. Harben.
Destroying Angel, The. By Louis Joseph Vance.
Dixie Hart. By Will N. Harben.
Double Traitor, The. By E. Phillips Oppenheim.
Drusilla With a Million. By Elizabeth Cooper.

Eagle of the Empire, The. By Cyrus Townsend Brady.
El Dorado. By Baroness Orczy.
Elusive Isabel. By Jacques Futrelle.
Empty Pockets. By Rupert Hughes.
Enchanted Hat, The. By Harold MacGrath.
Eye of Dread, The. By Payne Erskine.
Eyes of the World, The. By Harold Bell Wright.

Felix O'Day. By F. Hopkinson Smith.
50-40 or Fight. By Emerson Hough.
Fighting Chance, The. By Robert W. Chambers.
Financier, The. By Theodore Dreiser.
Flamsted Quarries. By Mary E. Waller.
Flying Mercury, The. By Eleanor M. Ingram.
For a Maiden Brave. By Chauncey C. Hotchkiss.
Four Million, The. By O. Henry.
Four Pool's Mystery, The. By Jean Webster.
Fruitful Vine, The. By Robert Hichens.

Get-Rich-Quick Wallingford. By George Randolph Chester.
Gilbert Neal. By Will N. Harben.
Girl From His Town, The. By Marie Van Vorst.
Girl of the Blue Ridge, A. By Payne Erskine.
Girl Who Lived in the Woods, The. By Marjorie Benton
    Cook.
Girl Who Won, The. By Beth Ellis.
Glory of Clementina, The. By Wm. J. Locke.
Glory of the Conquered, The. By Susan Glaspell.
God's Country and the Woman. By James Oliver Curwood.
God's Good Man. By Marie Corelli.
Going Some. By Rex Beach.
Gold Bag, The. By Carolyn Wells.

Popular Copyright Novels

AT MODERATE PRICES

Ask Your Dealer for a Complete List of
A. L. Burt Company's Popular Copyright Fiction

Golden Slipper, The. By Anna Katharine Green.
Golden Web, The. By Anthony Partridge.
Gordon Craig. By Randall Parrish.
Greater Love Hath No Man. By Frank L. Packard.
Greyfriars Bobby. By Eleanor Atkinson.
Guests of Hercules, The. By C. N. & A. M. Williamson.

Halcyone. By Elinor Glyn.
Happy Island (Sequel to Uncle William). By Jeannette Lee.
Havoc. By E. Phillips Oppenheim.
Heart of Philura, The. By Florence Kingsley.
Heart of the Desert, The. By Honoré Willsie.
Heart of the Hills, The. By John Fox, Jr.
Heart of the Sunset. By Rex Beach.
Heart of Thunder Mountain, The. By Elfrid A. Bingham.
Heather-Moon, The. By C. N. and A. M. Williamson .
Her Weight in Gold. By Geo. B. McCutcheon.
Hidden Children, The. By Robert W. Chambers.
Hoosier Volunteer, The. By Kate and Virgil D. Boyles.
Hopalong Cassidy. By Clarence E. Mulford.
How Leslie Loved. By Anne Warner.
Hugh Wynne, Free Quaker. By S. Weir Mitchell, M.D.
Husbands of Edith, The. By George Barr McCutcheon.

I Conquered. By Harold Titus.
Illustrious Prince, The. By E. Phillips Oppenheim.
Idols. By William J. Locke.
Indifference of Juliet, The. By Grace S. Richmond.
Inez. (Ill. Ed.) By Augusta J. Evans.
Infelice. By Augusta Evans Wilson.
In Her Own Right. By John Reed Scott.
Initials Only. By Anna Katharine Green.
In Another Girl's Shoes. By Berta Ruck.
Inner Law, The. By Will N. Harben.
Innocent. By Marie Corelli.
Insidious Dr. Fu-Manchu, The. By Sax Rohmer.
In the Brooding Wild. By Ridgwell Cullum.
Intrigues, The. By Harold Bindloss.
Iron Trail, The. By Rex Beach.
Iron Woman, The. By Margaret Deland.
Ishmael. (Ill.) By Mrs. Southworth.

Popular Copyright Novels

AT MODERATE PRICES

Ask Your Dealer for a Complete List of
A. L. Burt Company's Popular Copyright Fiction

Island of Regeneration, The. By Cyrus Townsend Brady.
Island of Surprise, The. By Cyrus Townsend Brady.

Japonette. By Robert W. Chambers.
Jean of the Lazy A. By B. M. Bower.
Jeanne of the Marshes. By E. Phillips Oppenheim.
Jennie Gerhardt. By Theodore Dreiser.
Joyful Heatherby. By Payne Erskine.
Jude the Obscure. By Thomas Hardy.
Judgment House, The. By Gilbert Parker.

Keeper of the Door, The. By Ethel M. Dell.
Keith of the Border. By Randall Parrish.
Kent Knowles: Quahaug. By Joseph C. Lincoln.
King Spruce. By Holman Day.
Kingdom of Earth, The. By Anthony Partridge.
Knave of Diamonds, The. By Ethel M. Dell.
Lady and the Pirate, The. By Emerson Hough.
Lady Merton, Colonist. By Mrs. Humphrey Ward.

Landloper, The. By Holman Day.
Land of Long Ago, The. By Eliza Calvert Hall.
Last Try, The. By John Reed Scott.
Last Shot, The. By Frederick N. Palmer.
Last Trail, The. By Zane Grey.
Laughing Cavalier, The. By Baroness Orczy.
Law Breakers, The. By Ridgwell Cullum.
Lighted Way, The. By E. Phillips Oppenheim.
Lighting Conductor Discovers America, The. By C. N. &
      A. N. Williamson.
Lin McLean. By Owen Wister.
Little Brown Jug at Kildare, The. By Meredith Nicholson.
Lone Wolf, The. By Louis Joseph Vance.
Long Roll, The. By Mary Johnson.
Lonesome Land. By B. M. Bower.
Lord Loveland Discovers America. By C. N. and A. M.
      Williamson.
Lost Ambassador. By E. Phillips Oppenheim.
Lost Prince, The. By Frances Hodgson Burnett.
Lost Road, The. By Richard Harding Davis.
Love Under Fire. By Randall Parrish.

Popular Copyright Novels

AT MODERATE PRICES

Ask Your Dealer for a Complete List of
A. L. Burt Company's Popular Copyright Fiction

Macaria. (Ill. Ed.) By Augusta J. Evans.
Maids of Paradise, The. By Robert W. Chambers.
Maid of the Forest, The. By Randall Parrish.
Maid of the Whispering Hills, The. By Vingie E. Roe.
Making of Bobby Burnit, The. By Randolph Chester.
Making Money. By Owen Johnson.
Mam' Linda. By Will N. Harben.
Man Outside, The. By Wyndham Martyn.
Man Trail, The. By Henry Oyen.
Marriage. By H. G. Wells.
Marriage of Theodora, The. By Mollie Elliott Seawell.
Mary Moreland. By Marie Van Vorst.
Master Mummer, The. By E. Phillips Oppenheim.
Max. By Katherine Cecil Thurston.
Maxwell Mystery, The. By Caroline Wells.
Mediator, The. By Roy Norton.
Memoirs of Sherlock Holmes. By A. Conan Doyle.
Mischief Maker, The. By E. Phillips Oppenheim.
Miss Gibbie Gault. By Kate Langley Bosher.
Miss Philura's Wedding Gown. By Florence Morse Kingsley.
Molly McDonald. By Randall Parrish.
Money Master, The. By Gilbert Parker.
Money Moon, The. By Jeffery Farnol.
Motor Maid, The. By C. N and A. M. Williamson.
Moth, The. By William Dana Orcutt.
Mountain Girl, The. By Payne Erskine.
Mr. Bingle. By George Barr McCutcheon.
Mr. Grex of Monte Carlo. By E. Phillips Oppenheim.
Mr. Pratt. By Joseph C. Lincoln.
Mr. Pratt's Patients. By Joseph C. Lincoln.
Mrs. Balfame. By Gertrude Atherton.
Mrs. Red Pepper. By Grace S. Richmond.
My Demon Motor Boat. By George Fitch.
My Friend the Chauffeur. By C. N. and A. M. Williamson.
My Lady Caprice. By Jeffery Farnol.
My Lady of Doubt. By Randall Parrish.
My Lady of the North, By Randall Parrish.
My Lady of the South. By Randall Parrish.

Ne'er-Do-Well, The. By Rex Beach.
Net, The. By Rex Beach.

Popular Copyright Novels

AT MODERATE PRICES

Ask Your Dealer for a Complete List of
A. L. Burt Company's Popular Copyright Fiction

New Clarion. By Will N. Harben.
Night Riders, The. By Ridgwell Cullum.
Night Watches. By W. W. Jacobs.
Nobody. By Louis Joseph Vance.

Once Upon a Time. By Richard Harding Davis.
One Braver Thing. By Richard Dehan.
One Way Trail, The. By Ridgwell Cullum.
Otherwise Phyllis. By Meredith Nicholson.

Pardners. By Rex Beach.
Parrott & Co. By Harold MacGrath.
Partners of the Tide. By Joseph C. Lincoln.
Passionate Friends, The. By H. G. Wells.
Patrol of the Sun Dance Trail, The. By Ralph Connor.
Paul Anthony, Christian. By Hiram W. Hayes.
Perch of the Devil. By Gertrude Atherton.
Peter Ruff. By E. Phillips Oppenheim.
People's Man, A. By E. Phillips Oppenheim.
Phillip Steele. By James Oliver Curwood.
Pidgin Island. By Harold MacGrath.
Place of Honeymoon, The. By Harold MacGrath.
Plunderer, The. By Roy Norton.
Pole Baker. By Will N. Harben.
Pool of Flame, The. By Louis Joseph Vance.
Port of Adventure, The. By C. N. and A. M. Williamson.
Postmaster, The. By Joseph C. Lincoln.
Power and the Glory, The. By Grace McGowan Cooke.
Prairie Wife, The. By Arthur Stringer.
Price of Love, The. By Arnold Bennett.
Price of the Prairie, The. By Margaret Hill McCarter.
Prince of Sinners. By A. E. Phillips Oppenheim.
Princes Passes, The. By C. N. and A. M. Williamson.
Princess Virginia, The. By C. N. and A. N. Williamson.
Promise, The. By J. B. Hendryx.
Purple Parasol, The. By Geo. B. McCutcheon.

Ranch at the Wolverine, The. By B. M. Bower.
Ranching for Sylvia. By Harold Bindloss.
Real Man, The. By Francis Lynde.
Reason Why, The. By Elinor Glyn.

Popular Copyright Novels

AT MODERATE PRICES

Ask Your Dealer for a Complete List of
A. L. Burt Company's Popular Copyright Fiction

Red Cross Girl, The. By Richard Harding Davis.
Red Mist, The. By Randall Parrish.
Redemption of Kenneth Galt, The. By Will N. Harben.
Red Lane, The. By Holman Day.
Red Mouse. The. By Wm. Hamilton Osborne.
Red Pepper Burns. By Grace S. Richmond.
Rejuvenation of Aunt Mary, The. By Anne Warner.
Return of Tarzan, The. By Edgar Rice Burroughs.
Riddle of Night, The. By Thomas W. Hanshew.
Rim of the Desert, The. By Ada Woodruff Anderson.
Rise of Roscoe Paine, The. By J. C. Lincoln.
Road to Providence, The. By Maria Thompson Daviess.
Robinetta. By Kate Douglas Wiggin.
Rocks of Valpré, The. By Ethel M. Dell.
Rogue by Compulsion, A. By Victor Bridges.
Rose in the Ring, The. By George Barr McCutcheon.
Rose of the World. By Agnes and Egerton Castle.
Rose of Old Harpeth, The. By Maria Thompson Daviess.
Round the Corner in Gay Street. By Grace S. Richmond.
Routledge Rides Alone. By Will L. Comfort.

St. Elmo. (Ill. Ed.) By Augusta J. Evans.
Salamander, The. By Owen Johnson.
Scientific Sprague. By Francis Lynde.
Second Violin, The. By Grace S. Richmond.
Secret of the Reef, The. By Harold Bindloss.
Secret History. By C. N. & A. M. Williamson.
Self-Raised. (Ill.) By Mrs. Southworth.
Septimus. By William J. Locke.
Set in Silver. By C. N. and A. M. Williamson.
Seven Darlings, The. By Gouverneur Morris.
Shea of the Irish Brigade. By Randall Parrish.
Shepherd of the Hills, The. By Harold Bell Wright.
Sheriff of Dyke Hole, The. By Ridgwell Cullum.
Sign at Six, The. By Stewart Edw. White.
Silver Horde, The. By Rex Beach.
Simon the Jester. By William J. Locke.
Siren of the Snows, A. By Stanley Shaw.
Sir Richard Calmady. By Lucas Malet.
Sixty-First Second, The. By Owen Johnson.
Slim Princess, The. By George Ade.

Popular Copyright Novels

AT MODERATE PRICES

Ask Your Dealer for a Complete List of
A. L. Burt Company's Popular Copyright Fiction

Soldier of the Legion, A. By C. N. and A. M. Williamson.
Somewhere in France. By Richard Harding Davis.
Speckled Bird, A. By Augusta Evans Wilson.
Spirit in Prison, A. By Robert Hichens.
Spirit of the Border, The. By Zane Grey.
Splendid Chance, The. By Mary Hastings Bradley.
Spoilers, The. By Rex Beach.
Spragge's Canyon. By Horace Annesley Vachell.
Still Jim. By Honoré Willsie.
Story of Foss River Ranch, The. By Ridgwell Cullum.
Story of Marco, The. By Eleanor H. Porter.
Strange Disappearance, A. By Anna Katherine Green.
Strawberry Acres. By Grace S. Richmond.
Streets of Ascalon, The. By Robert W. Chambers.
Sunshine Jane. By Anne Warner.
Susan Clegg and Her Friend Mrs. Lathrop. By Anne Warner.
Sword of the Old Frontier, A. By Randall Parrish.

Tales of Sherlock Holmes. By A. Conan Doyle.
Taming of Zenas Henry, The. By Sara Ware Bassett.
Tarzan of the Apes. By Edgar R. Burroughs.
Taste of Apples, The. By Jennette Lee.
Tempting of Tavernake, The. By E. Phillips Oppenheim.
Tess of the D'Urbervilles. By Thomas Hardy.
Thankful Inheritance. By Joseph C. Lincoln.
That Affair Next Door. By Anna Katharine Green.
That Printer of Udell's. By Harold Bell Wright.
Their Yesterdays. By Harold Bell Wright.
The Side of the Angels. By Basil King.
Throwback, The. By Alfred Henry Lewis.
Thurston of Orchard Valley. By Harold Bindloss.
To M. L. G.; or, He Who Passed. By Anon.
Trail of the Axe, The. By Ridgwell Cullum.
Trail of Yesterday, The. By Chas. A. Seltzer.
Treasure of Heaven, The. By Marie Corelli.
Truth Dexter. By Sidney McCall.
T. Tembarom. By Frances Hodgson Burnett.
Turbulent Duchess, The. By Percy J. Brebner.

Popular Copyright Novels

AT MODERATE PRICES

Ask Your Dealer for a Complete List of
A. L. Burt Company's Popular Copyright Fiction

Twenty-fourth of June, The. By Grace S. Richmond.
Twins of Suffering Creek, The. By Ridgwell Cullum.
Two-Gun Man, The. By Charles A. Seltzer.

Uncle William. By Jeannette Lee.
Under the Country Sky. By Grace S. Richmond.
Unknown Mr. Kent, The. By Roy Norton.
"Unto Caesar." By Baronett Orczy.
Up From Slavery. By Booker T. Washington.

Valiants of Virginia, The. By Hallie Erminie Rives.
Valley of Fear, The. By Sir A. Conan Doyle.
Vane of the Timberlands. By Harold Bindloss.
Vanished Messenger, The. By E. Phillips Oppenheim.
Vashti. By Augusta Evans Wilson.
Village of Vagabonds, A. By F. Berkley Smith.
Visioning, The. By Susan Glaspell.

Wall of Men, A. By Margaret H. McCarter.
Wallingford in His Prime. By George Randolph Chester.
Wanted—A Chaperon. By Paul Leicester Ford.
Wanted—A Matchmaker. By Paul Leicester Ford.
Watchers of the Plains, The. By Ridgwell Cullum.
Way Home, The. By Basil King.
Way of an Eagle, The. By E. M. Dell.
Way of a Man, The. By Emerson Hough.
Way of the Strong, The. By Ridgwell Cullum.
Way of These Women, The. By E. Phillips Oppenheim.
Weavers, The. By Gilbert Parker.
West Wind, The. By Cyrus T. Brady.
When Wilderness Was King. By Randolph Parrish.
Where the Trail Divides. By Will Lillibridge.
Where There's a Will. By Mary R. Rinehart.
White Sister, The. By Marion Crawford.
White Waterfall, The. By James Francis Dwyer.
Who Goes There? By Robert W. Chambers.
Window at the White Cat, The. By Mary Roberts Rinehart.
Winning of Barbara Worth, The. By Harold Bell Wright.
Winning the Wilderness. By Margaret Hill McCarter.
With Juliet in England. By Grace S. Richmond.
Witness for the Defense, The. By A. E. W. Mason.

Popular Copyright Novels

AT MODERATE PRICES

Woman in Question, The. By John Reed Scott.
Woman Haters, The. By Joseph C. Lincoln.
Woman Thou Gavest Me, The. By Hall Caine.
Woodcarver of 'Lympus, The. By Mary E. Waller.
Woodfire in No. 3, The. By F. Hopkinson Smith.
Wooing of Rosamond Fayre, The. By Berta Ruck.

You Never Know Your Luck. By Gilbert Parker.
Younger Set, The. By Robert W. Chambers.